insight text guide

Anica Boulanger-Mashberg

Behind the Beautiful Forevers

Katherine Boo

First published in 2016, reprinted in 2017, 2018.

Insight Publications Pty Ltd
3/350 Charman Road
Cheltenham VIC 3192
Australia
Tel: +61 3 8571 4950
Fax: +61 3 8571 0257
Email: books@insightpublications.com.au

www.insightpublications.com.au

National Library of Australia Cataloguing-in-Publication entry:
Boulanger-Mashberg, Anica, author.
Katherine Boo's Behind the Beautiful Forevers / Anica Boulanger-Mashberg.
9781925316896 (paperback)
Insight text guide.
For secondary school age.
Boo, Katherine. Behind the beautiful forevers.
Boo, Katherine. –Criticism and interpretation.

Other ISBNs:
9781925316902 (digital)
9781925316919 (bundle: print + digital)

Cover design: The Modern Art Production Group

Printed in Australia

contents

CHARACTER MAP

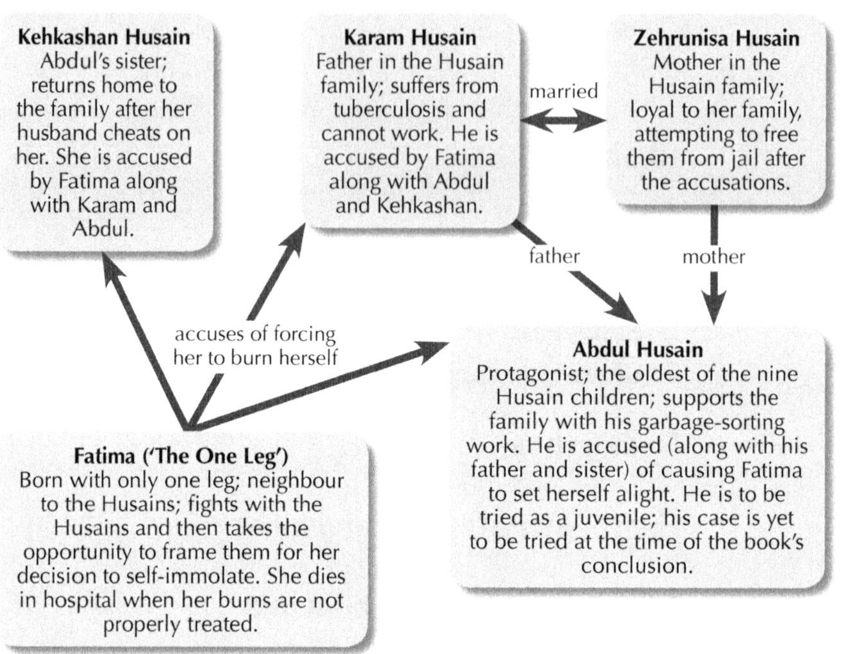

Meena
The fifteen-year-old daughter of Tamil parents who founded Annawadi; beaten by her family and forced to do all the housework; commits suicide.

Manju Waghekar
An obedient daughter; fulfils her duties at home, in college and as the teacher of the school run from her home. She hopes to become Annawadi's first female college graduate.

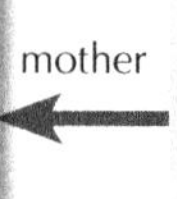

Asha Waghekar
Aspires to be, and becomes, the slumlord of Annawadi. She is more concerned about money and power than individuals' suffering.

OVERVIEW

About the author

American writer Katherine Boo was born in 1964 and studied at Columbia University. Boo has a background in journalistic writing, and her work has been published in magazines and newspapers, including *The Washington Post*. In 2003, she began working as a staff writer at *The New Yorker*, where she has published many long-form essays, most of which are investigative in style and explore experiences of poverty, disadvantage, social immobility and inequality in countries such as India and America. She won a National Magazine Award for Feature Writing for 'The Marriage Cure', one such article, in 2004. Other awards in her career include a Pulitzer Prize for Public Service awarded to *The Washington Post* for her series of articles about people living with intellectual disabilities. She has also won several other awards for her work, including a MacArthur Fellowship, a grant she used to help pay for surgery on her right hand – Boo suffers from rheumatoid arthritis and several immunological disorders, which she says helped to encourage 'a healthy respect for volatility' (McGrath 2012) and served as a motivator for her research into and writing about the experiences of those who are struggling with various social and political challenges to life.

Behind the Beautiful Forevers (2012) is Boo's first book, and was researched and written using a kind of 'immersion' style that she had already utilised many times in her journalism. The book won the 2012 National Book Award and many other prizes, and was a finalist for the Pulitzer Prize for Nonfiction in 2013. It has also been adapted for the stage by award-winning British playwright David Hare. The play premiered in London at the National Theatre in 2014, and was reviewed very positively.

Boo met Sunil Khilnani, the man she later married, while in India in 2001. Today, she divides her time between India and the United States.

She joined the Pulitzer Prize Board in 2014, and works as a staff writer for *The New Yorker* as well as continuing to pursue her research.

Synopsis

Behind the Beautiful Forevers presents a factual portrait of Annawadi, a Mumbai slum, through a close investigation of approximately two years in the lives of a handful of its residents. The text is divided into four sections (see 'Structure' in 'Genre, Structure & Language' for further discussion on the content of each section), and the narrative loosely follows the story of Abdul Husain and his family as they are accused of provoking their neighbour, Fatima, into self-immolation. The legal and court proceedings that follow are protracted and fraught with corruption and failures of the system to provide anything approaching a fair trial.

Presented alongside the Husains' story are the stories of a number of other Annawadians, contextualising the Husains' experience and painting a broad yet detailed picture of life in this particular slum. By extension, this is also a portrait of the Indian undercity, since the events in Annawadi are often described as not being unique to this particular slum.

Another of the main families is the Waghekars: Asha, her largely absent alcoholic husband and their daughter, Manju, and two sons, Rahul and Ganesh. Asha, an ambitious and independent woman, has designs on becoming the slumlord of Annawadi – an unusual but not unheard-of position for a woman. She works with the local Corporator in a mutually beneficial arrangement that is representative of the corrupt dealings present throughout all levels of Indian life. Her eldest, Manju, is a diligent daughter, student and teacher, striving to better herself through education.

Other significant characters include a collection of young Annawadians, many of whom (such as Kalu, Sonu and Sunil) are Abdul's fellow garbage-workers: scavengers and thieves who bring him the materials he then sorts and sells to recyclers.

Though the text follows a generally chronological progression, the plot shifts between various characters' points of view with each chapter (and sometimes also within chapters), creating a multilayered and interconnected portrait of the slum.

Character summaries

Abdul Hakim Husain

Abdul is a central character, aged roughly between sixteen and nineteen (his family don't know). The oldest of Karam and Zehrunisa's nine children, he maintains the family income through their garbage-sorting business. Along with his father and sister, he is accused of causing Fatima's death.

Karam Husain

Karam, husband of Zehrunisa and father of the Husain family, suffers from tuberculosis and cannot participate in the family business, leaving Abdul responsible for the physical labour. He dreams of moving the family away from the slum to a plot of land in Vasai, but lacks the capacity to make it happen. He can read in several languages.

Zehrunisa Husain

Wife of Karam and mother of Abdul and his eight siblings, Zehrunisa plays an active role in the family business because of her husband's illness, and is a loyal and strong woman who works hard to try to get her family out of jail after Fatima's immolation. She ensures that the family play an integral role in the small Muslim community in Annawadi.

Mirchi Husain

Abdul's younger brother Mirchi has no interest in the family business, dreaming of 'a clean job' (p.xvii). He struggles at school and prides himself on his laziness, but steps up to the responsibility of earning for the family after Abdul is accused and awaiting trial.

Kehkashan Husain

Kehkashan is the oldest Husain daughter. She returns home to Annawadi when she suspects her husband of cheating on her. She becomes involved in the verbal fight with Fatima and is subsequently put on trial along with her father.

Fatima ('The One Leg') Shaikh

Fatima, a Muslim like the Husains, lives next door to them and shares a wall. She was born with only one leg and uses crutches. Her parents married her to an older Hindu man, and the couple have had 'three scrawny girls' (p.xvi), one of whom drowned in a bucket when young (an accident for which some hold Fatima responsible). Fatima has had many affairs, compensating for a body and a marriage that have let her down. Often angry, Fatima makes the extreme decision to set herself alight when the Husains irritate her by renovating in their hut. She accuses them of making her do it, and later dies of an infection.

Asha Waghekar

A prominent figure in Annawadi, Asha aspires to be the slumlord, working with the local Corporator to help him hold political influence and therefore sharing in the benefits of his corruption. Asha's husband is an alcoholic, and she has raised their three teenage children with little assistance. A formidable opponent, Asha is capable of helping many Annawadians, but only does so for her own profit.

Manju Waghekar

Asha's daughter Manju is the only girl in the slum attending college, and is also hardworking and beautiful. She is a dutiful daughter but quietly disapproves of her mother's values.

Rahul Waghekar

Rahul, Asha's son, is Mirchi's best friend; he is cheerful and well liked. He manages to get regular work in the nearby airport hotels – a kind of employment to which Mirchi aspires.

Sunil Sharma

A young garbage scavenger, Sunil often works with others (including Abdul, Kalu and Sonu) in order to support himself and his sister Sunita. He is enterprising and energetic even as he doubts his place in the world.

Kalu

Fifteen-year-old Kalu (his real name is Deepak Rai; he is nicknamed Kalu for his dark skin) is the closest thing Abdul has to a friend. He is popular with the other slum boys, and even Zehrunisa is fond of him. He is a 'road boy' or a thief, and when he dies outside the airport his death is dismissed by the authorities and declared to be illness-related, though he was almost certainly murdered.

Meena

Fifteen-year-old Meena is the daughter of Tamil parents who helped build the slum. She is regularly beaten by her family, and expected to stay at home and do all the housework and cooking. A friend and confidante to Manju, Meena attempts suicide several times, desperate to escape a miserable life and the prospects of an even harder life as a young village wife, before succeeding.

Sanjay Shetty

The Sahar police threaten a group of road boys, including Sanjay, beating them and demanding they stay silent about Kalu's death, lest they be accused of murder. Although he is a minor character, Sanjay's response – suicide – is significant, illustrating the pressures of slum life and the limited options slum-dwellers face.

Poornima Paikrao

A minor recurring character, Poornima is a government special executive officer, assigned to the legal case between Fatima and the Husains. She regularly attempts to extort the Husains – for example, by threatening to alter testimonies to the Husains' detriment if they refuse to pay her. She represents the embedded corruption in the government.

The Master

A minor character, The Master is a teacher at the Dongri juvenile detention centre, where Abdul spends time awaiting his trial. The Master is an almost mystical leader figure in Abdul's mind, inspiring him to a life of moral behaviour.

Sonu Gupta

Another of the young boys of Annawadi, Sonu is one of the most successful of the scavengers. He is also moral in his work practices, such as when he lets Sunil work with him, dividing the profits equally. Such attitudes are rare in the culture of corruption Boo portrays.

Subhash Sawant

Subhash is the Corporator of Ward 76 (containing Annawadi) for most of the text. A member of the right-wing Shiv Sena sect along with Asha, he has a close working relationship with her, relying on her to uphold his reputation in the slum, and in turn providing her access to various schemes and deals.

BACKGROUND & CONTEXT

Cultural context

India is a heavily populated country – the second-most populated in the world, after China – with a fast-growing economy, but a highly disproportionate distribution of social and financial capital between the upper classes and the underprivileged. As Boo observes in her Author's Note, India, at the time at which the events in *Behind the Beautiful Forevers* took place, accounted for a third of the world's poverty. The gap between the wealthy and the poor paves the way for slums such as Annawadi to lie beside symbols of the city's developing wealth, such as the airport and expensive hotels.

The environmental juxtaposition of two such different lifestyles echoes the contrasts between the prospects for the wealthy and the struggles of the poor. This is compounded by the complex caste system in India, described by Boo as 'the most artfully oppressive division of labour ever devised' (p.42). The Indian caste system has historically divided the citizens into class groups that define individuals' identities by connecting them permanently and forcibly to particular levels of society. An individual inherits their caste membership from their family, and it is an inescapable stamp that determines their employment opportunities and therefore their future. This system ensures that the gap between wealth and poverty remains vast.

In *Behind the Beautiful Forevers*, the caste system is not foregrounded in the examination of Annawadi, as all the slum-dwellers are obviously lower-caste members. However, even within the lower castes, there is a hierarchy; for example, Meena's family is described as being from the Dalit caste, also known as the 'untouchables' – a caste at the very bottom of the hierarchy. Although the text suggests that for younger characters such as Meena and Manju, caste divisions are considered a much less significant factor in one's fate, friendships and future, there are clear indications that the system still has a very powerful hold over the social structure of the country. In rural areas such as the village where Asha's family come from, for example, Dalits are still considered 'contaminated': if a Dalit 'touched a cup', the cup would have to be 'destroyed' (p.183).

Slum life

Increasing overpopulation and a lack of affordable housing in India – particularly in big cities such as Mumbai, where many rural citizens travel in the hopes of finding work – have contributed to the development of slums: areas where poor people live, usually in temporary or roughly constructed huts, because they have no alternative. In most cases, slums are settled on land owned by someone else (much like Annawadi, which is on airport-owned land), so as illegal residences, they lack facilities such as waste management and sanitation, running water and electricity. In addition to the limited resources and physical infrastructure, overcrowding and competition for space intensify the difficulties of living in such areas. There is also little or no security, as governments and private landowners regularly clear slums and often develop the land instead (as begins to occur towards the end of *Behind the Beautiful Forevers*), leaving slum-dwellers with nowhere to go but other already overcrowded slums.

In *Behind the Beautiful Forevers,* Boo portrays residents' hopes that they will manage to improve their living situation by securing for themselves relocation to marginally improved dwellings in permanent apartment blocks – as per agreements with the developers and government. However, the text also illustrates the near impossibility of actually succeeding in this endeavour, as delays, corruption, bribery and politically motivated misappropriation of funds and resources preclude such arrangements ever coming to fruition.

Many slums operate under a social arrangement such as that in Annawadi, where a 'slumlord' holds power within the slum, often in exchange for answering to the local elected political member, or Corporator. Boo presents a detailed examination of the mutually beneficial relationship between Asha and Corporator Subhash Sawant (see Chapter 2 particularly). However, despite the power afforded her within Annawadi due to her position, Asha is still heavily indebted and obliged to the Corporator, so her power is very limited.

Religion

India is home to many different religious communities, including Hindus, Buddhists, Christians and Muslims. The vast majority of Indians are Hindu, with Islam the dominant of the minority religions. Most of the characters in *Behind the Beautiful Forevers* identify as Hindus, while the Husain family are a strong presence among the Muslim minority (roughly one in ten) in Annawadi.

Religion is not a central focus of Boo's text, but it is an underlying element in many relationships and events:

- The conflict between Fatima and the Husains is made all the more painful because they share a Muslim identity, bonding over their faith in a community heavily dominated by Hindus.
- The Muslim terrorists who attack Mumbai add fear during Abdul's difficult time, as he expects retaliation against not only the wider Muslim community but also his immediate family.
- Several characters have an ambivalent relationship with their faith, participating in religious activity more for appearance than anything else, and this undermines their ability to maintain confidence and self-identity.

Although Boo does show that the Husains suffer some discrimination as a result of their religion, she also indicates that this is not the sole source of their problems. They are equally discriminated against and resented for their ability to earn a significant income in the slum; and within the wider Indian context (such as in the legal proceedings), their poverty is responsible for as much of their ill treatment at the hands of superiors and officials as their religion.

Political system

India is a democracy; although, as Boo's text shows, governmental corruption is so rife and blatant that the 'democratic' electoral system is almost farcical, and the government remains 'dysfunctional' (p.216). Boo provides various pieces of evidence for the argument that there is no fair democratic process, such as:

- the fact that Asha's family have two voter registration cards each, while others, such as the Husains or the eunuchs, are unable to vote because their registrations are not valid (they have not been processed)
- the pressure on Asha to support a new political party when there is a new Corporator for the ward soon before the elections
- the attempted bribe of sewer covers from the Congress Party before the election, which is retracted and offered to a larger slum.

The influence of political corruption is shown to be an enduring pressure on the lives of Annawadians, whether directly – for characters such as Asha, who have a relationship with the local Corporator – or indirectly, as all the slum-dwellers' lives are shaped by what those in power choose to do with slum resources and land.

Research methodology

Boo has a background in investigative journalism, and her preferred method of research is a style known as 'immersive' research and reporting. She discusses this briefly in her Author's Note, as well as in many sources beyond the text (see 'References & Reading' for a link to a Radio National interview with Katherine Boo about her work and her process). The technique requires extensive investigation, involving spending hundreds of hours over an extended period of time – in this case, more than three years – with her subjects in their own environment. This allows for great detail in the resulting text: Boo documented Annawadi and its residents in text, photographs, videos and audio recordings, and therefore amassed a vast bank of information to draw on in constructing *Behind the Beautiful Forevers*.

Boo had made an earlier attempt to write a book that examined such socioeconomic situations within her home country – the United States – but she could not complete it because some of her subjects became unavailable during the project. This is one potential outcome of the kind of 'immersion journalism' Boo also undertook for her book about a Mumbai slum: the resulting text is heavily dictated by the realities of the situation, including individuals' willingness to participate and the playing out of real events. For example, in *Behind the Beautiful Forevers*, readers never learn the outcome of Abdul's trial, as it was not completed during the time Boo spent in Annawadi. When you analyse the text, consider these restrictions on its content and shape, and the resulting influence on readers' understanding and interpretation of the characters and themes. For example, because Boo could not report Abdul's conviction or acquittal, readers are left without a summing up of his guilt or innocence from an external perspective. This allows them to form their own conclusions about the character, based on what the text has presented.

One way to overcome some of the restrictions of the immersive process is to also consult extensive documents and archives, as Boo did, in order to expand on and validate the story she was able to uncover through her research. In her text, she rarely differentiates between the sources of information – except in specific instances, such as Kalu's death, where she contrasts the actual event, as experienced by individuals, with the official records constructed to explain it. This integration of lived experience with 'official' documentation has the effect of legitimising eyewitness experience, encouraging readers to form strong connections with the characters and the issues they present.

While Boo is careful to keep her first-person experience as a writer in the background rather than the foreground of the text, she has acknowledged in an interview published on her website for the book that 'a reporter's presence is bound to change things' (see 'References' for source details).

GENRE, STRUCTURE & LANGUAGE

Genre

Behind the Beautiful Forevers is a work of **nonfiction**: its characters, locations and events reflect actual characters, locations and events in the real world, rather than presenting creations from the author's imagination. However, the details reported in the book are mediated through the author's writing, so they are still shaped, interpreted and framed by particular biases (both intentional and unintentional). Although Abdul is a real person, for example, the Abdul presented in the book is also a literary character, and is constructed through Boo's authorial decisions, in the same way a character in a work of fiction is constructed.

Authors of fiction and nonfiction are faced with many of the same decisions regarding language use, structure and characterisation; in nonfiction, just as in fiction, the events and details reported in the text are all conscious decisions of the author. In nonfiction, unlike in fiction, authors are restricted by the constraints of reality, meaning that they cannot invent plot developments or character traits, but they have the power to be selective about what they include and in what order or context they present it, so they are able to manipulate readers' responses and understanding of particular characters, relationships, themes, ideas and values. Authors of nonfiction do not simply record facts; they shape them in order to present particular perspectives on events and ideas.

Some of the techniques used by Boo in *Behind the Beautiful Forevers* are more common to genres other than nonfiction, such as fiction and poetry. These techniques include:

- language choices, such as the use of rich figurative language
- structural techniques, such as the chapter and section divisions and titles, which are often lyrical and weighted with symbolic meaning
- other elements such as the third-person narrative perspective (with the exception of the Author's Note) – a common point of view for

nonfiction, but it is also subtly aligned with different characters in different chapters in a way that is more akin to fiction.

Such techniques in nonfiction are associated with a form known as **creative nonfiction**, sometimes **literary nonfiction** or **narrative nonfiction**. Lee Gutkind, one of the leading writers and scholars of the form, defines creative nonfiction (in the journal of the same title, which he founded) very simply as 'true stories well told'. Several of the reviews cited on the back cover of *Behind the Beautiful Forevers* offer terms other than creative nonfiction to describe the text, such as 'a non-fiction novel' and 'documentary storytelling'. All these descriptions emphasise the fact that two aspects of Boo's text are equally important: the literary construction, or craft, and the factual material she is reporting. When you are analysing the book, remember to keep both these elements in mind as you discuss characters, themes and ideas.

However, despite use of 'literary' techniques common to works of fiction, in other ways the text is strongly representative of nonfiction: it is realistic, naturalistic and largely chronological. There are limitations to the 'creative' licence allowed when writing creative nonfiction.

Structure

Behind the Beautiful Forevers is divided into chapters, and the chapters into sections, allowing Boo to gather various types of narrative information into larger frameworks, and encouraging readers to identify commonalities between the characters and stories presented in individual chapters. Below is a brief summary of these sections.

Divisions

Prologue

The prologue draws readers into the narrative at a key point of climax: the events immediately following the burning of Fatima, 'The One Leg'. By beginning at a crisis point for Abdul, one of the central characters, Boo not only attracts her audience's interest and curiosity immediately but also sets the scene for the rest of the text, and sketches Abdul's personal qualities and his relationships with his family – all of which will be elaborated on later.

Part One: Undercitizens

The first section comprises an introductory chapter about Annawadi, followed by three chapters each titled with the name of one of the central characters in the text. The focus in each chapter on a particular character and their experience of slum life allows Boo to present a detailed portrait of the challenges and restrictions present in all Annawadians' lives, providing a background for the events explored in Part Two.

Part Two: The Business of Burning

These four chapters narrow the portrait of Annawadi life to concentrate on the Husain family and their particular goals, values and relationships. This encourages readers to empathise with the family during Fatima's traumatic immolation and the equally disturbing aftermath as the Husains are accused, jailed and even extorted.

Part Three: A Little Wildness

The focus is widened again, like a camera panning back to reveal a broader scene around a close-up shot, to further explore other Annawadi characters – particularly younger characters such as Manju, Sonu, Sunil, Kalu and Sanjay. This is in order to contextualise Abdul's experience, and some of the broader themes of the text, such as poverty, hopelessness and corruption.

Part Four: Up and Out

The longest section, Part Four draws together the narratives introduced in the earlier sections, including Abdul's and his family's suffering and struggles after the burning, and the difficulties of life for young Annawadians. The final chapter in the section looks towards the future of Annawadi and its residents, as the airport authorities begin to reclaim the slumlands.

Author's Note

This final short section contextualises the book by explaining some of the motivation, decisions and processes that went into its construction. This helps readers understand the characters and themes in more depth and encourages them to reflect on various aspects of the text. For example, Boo discusses common public misconceptions of slum-dwellers as either 'mythic' or 'pathetic' (p.249), arguing that what she encountered in Annawadi was entirely unlike these stereotypes. This positions readers to assess the portrayal Boo has offered, and find a more complex understanding of all the characters in the text.

Chronology

While much of the text progresses in a linear chronology, there are several important digressions. The principle one is the prologue, in which Boo begins the book with an event from the middle of the narrative timeline. In addition to the practical impact of attracting readers and connecting them with the text quickly, this technique reflects the 'literary' element of the genre, introducing readers to the tone and style of the book, and indicating from the outset that although the book is a recording of facts, it also aspires to provide a satisfying narrative through the use of literary techniques.

For example, consider the first few sentences of Chapter 1. Boo manipulates readers' experience of chronology as well as the 'reality' of the narrative: she invites us to 'rewind' and to see one of the main characters 'running backward' (p.3) through the events described in the previous chapter, in order to approach aspects of the story from a different perspective and point in time. This not only provides a stimulating approach to the presentation of factual information but also encourages readers to take an active role in interpreting the events and characters to come.

Language

The official languages of India are English and Hindi, but in Mumbai, where the text is set (and in the state of Maharashtra, where characters, including Asha, come from), Marathi is the official language. Note that Urdu, often referred to in *Behind the Beautiful Forevers*, is a form of Hindi. Many Indians – including many in this text – are multilingual: that is, fluent in two or more languages or dialects. Others are less fluent, but still manage to get by in a second language, such as when Abdul has to make a concerted effort to follow the Marathi conversations when he is first imprisoned (Chapter 7).

Boo has included many words from Indian languages, particularly when they are not easily translated into a single English word or concept – for example, *maidan* (p.x) or *purdah* (p.75). These terms are almost always contextualised or defined at their first usage so that readers are not expected to research beyond the text or have any existing knowledge of the culture. This makes the text accessible to a broad audience, while retaining a strong connection with Indian culture and languages.

Although the book was written in English, much of the dialogue in the text has been translated; in her Author's Note, Boo credits the Annawadi women who helped her conduct her research by translating for her, often providing their own thoughts and opinions while doing so. Boo does not usually specify which language her characters speak, though on some occasions it is a key feature in the text, notably when exchanges take place in languages or dialects that may not be the characters' primary. Examples include:

- Manju studying canonical English texts for school
- Kehkashan struggling to understand some of what is going on during her court case, because they are speaking in Marathi
- Karam reading Urdu newspapers.

In other instances, shared language may be a marker of shared cultural, social or religious identities and experiences, such as when Boo notes that Asha and Mr Kamble watch 'the same Marathi-language channel' on television (p.29).

Style

As discussed in 'Genre', Boo uses many literary techniques, including language that is often descriptive, figurative and symbolic. For example, at the end of the chapter recounting Fatima's burning, there is the simile 'the sky above the maidan purple as a bruise' (p.98), which describes the physical environment but also echoes the mood and the psychological damage recently done within the community. Such language choices help the text achieve a poetic style.

The style also remains formal throughout, in keeping with the journalistic, nonfiction aspect of the text. However, dialogue often uses a more informal register, as the direct speech reflects characters' everyday speech patterns, and may include slang, coarse language, nicknames, omission or irregular rhythms. This brings a sense of realism, helping readers to engage with the world of the text and empathise with the characters, in turn understanding their dilemmas and the underlying values these represent.

Narrative voice

Boo actively avoids the first-person perspective, writing in the third person – though often a 'limited' third-person perspective (aligned particularly with the experiences, opinions and understanding of one character). In removing the 'I' of the investigative reporter, Boo focuses the reader's attention on the experiences of the characters, rather than providing an external interpretation of them.

CHAPTER-BY-CHAPTER ANALYSIS

Prologue: 'Between Roses' (pp.ix–xxii)

Summary: *17 July 2008, Mumbai. Abdul hides for the night in his garbage-sorting shed; the text provides background information on Annawadi and its residents, including the Husains; Karam is arrested; Abdul surrenders at the police station.*

Chapter 1 begins after the event that forms the narrative heart of *Behind the Beautiful Forevers*: the burning of Fatima and the resulting persecutions of Abdul and his family. This is a point of increased tension for many of the central characters, so beginning the narrative here draws readers quickly in to the vivid and visceral world of Annawadi.

As well as offering a preliminary sketch (physical and psychological) of one of the book's central characters, the prologue introduces us to the physical environment in which much of the narrative takes place: the detailed descriptions of the 'bedlam' that is the norm each evening in the maidan (p.x), and of the contents of Abdul's garbage shed (p.xi), create rich and evocative portraits of the noisy, filthy, crowded, vibrant atmosphere of the slum. The descriptions are not only visual but also rely on other senses, such as in the evocation of the 'stink of trash and the fear-sweat that befouled Abdul's clothing' (p.xiii). This immerses readers powerfully in the world the Husains inhabit, providing context for the Husain family history and dynamics that are also described.

In contrast to these images of Annawadi's poverty and filth are the descriptions of various Annawadians' dreams for better futures – clean jobs, bigger houses, education, improvements to health. This is an enduring theme in the text.

Finally, the prologue offers a sociopolitical overview of the Annawadi slum and its context within India's swift-growing economy. As Abdul's little brother Mirchi puts it, they are the lowest of the low, but surrounded by the opposite extreme of wealth and social standing, with the slum lying beside the expensive airport hotels outside the Mumbai international airport terminal.

Key point

The prologue states that Abdul and the Husains did not burn Fatima (p.xix); providing a clear argument that they are being pursued unfairly, and indicating that the intention of the text is more to convey facts and describe situations than to encourage any 'detective' work on the part of readers.

Key vocabulary

Maidan: an Indian word for an urban open space, often used (in towns, not slums) for markets.

Q What other important themes and ideas are introduced in this prologue?

Q Why do you think Boo uses a prologue instead of containing all this material in the first chapter?

PART ONE: UNDERCITIZENS

Chapter 1: Annawadi (pp.3–16)

Summary: *Abdul sorts garbage on the maidan; Rahul boasts about his work at the hotel; Abdul sells the garbage; the plot of land at Vasai is first mentioned.*

The chapter covers a day in Abdul's life, seven months prior to Fatima's burning. This involves him being woken early and rudely by his mother, sorting garbage all day, listening to his brother Mirchi's best friend Rahul discuss working at rich parties in a nearby hotel and, finally, taking his garbage to nearby slum Saki Naka to sell to the recyclers. The descriptions again emphasise the sights and dangers of slum life, contrasting this experience with the world of wealth at the Intercontinental hotel, where Rahul has a few days' work. However, despite the contrast (such as is represented in Rahul's descriptions of the nice toilets, the ice sculptures, the women and the clothes), the chapter also identifies similarities – at the New Year's Eve party, Rahul observes that the rich were 'just people drinking and dancing and standing around acting stupid, like people here do every night' (p.11). While the differences in lifestyle afforded to the rich over the poor are huge, the chapter shows that differences in behaviour are often not significant.

The chapter concludes with a mention of the plot of land in Vasai that is 'the Husains' latest plan of escape from Annawadi' (p.4). This introduces a central motif in the book: the idea of escape from the claustrophobia and hopelessness of the slum.

Q How does Rahul's attempt to rescue the kite symbolise themes and ideas of the text?

Chapter 2: Asha (pp.17–30)

Summary: *The slumlord system is explained, and Asha's role in the Annawadi community is described in detail. Asha receives visits from her neighbours.*

Asha, whose position and ambitions were introduced in the previous chapter, is constructed as force to be reckoned with:

- She has raised her three children with little or no help from her alcoholic husband (p.18).
- She has made connections with the Corporator (the local elected official) and has already been rewarded for her political service to him and Shiv Sena with temp work at the kindergarten, which is a 'sinecure': or a position that offers a much greater return than it demands in commitment (p.19).
- She is the first and last to speak to the current slumlord, Robert Pires, aggressively and defensively (p.19).
- She is wily, figuring out how to take advantage of a society where she sees every individual 'blame his dissatisfaction on someone else' and 'everyone, everywhere, complained about their neighbours' (p.20).

Asha plays an important role in the story later, when Abdul's family turn to her for help after the arrests. This chapter sets up her power and position early, explaining how and why she has gotten to where she is, and how others depend on her. It also hints at her reluctance to be involved with the Husains: we learn that she dislikes both Fatima and Zehrunisa, considering their conflicts petty.

Q Do you think Boo presents Asha as admirable or contemptible? Support your response with evidence from this chapter.

Q How are Asha and Abdul similar? How do they differ?

Chapter 3: Sunil (pp.31–49)

Summary: *Sunil and Sunita return to Annawadi from the orphanage; Sunil scavenges on the wall above the Mithi River; Zehrunisa ejects their tenants after the riots; the airport management is poised to destroy Annawadi and the other airport slums; Sunil goes on a successful stealing mission with Kalu.*

The third chapter offers a glimpse of another survivor in Annawadi: Sunil, and also his father and sister, contributing to the growing portrait of a vibrant slum full of complex family dramas.

Sunil is useful to Kalu when they go to retrieve the stolen iron in the middle of the night, and he feels honoured to have been given the job. Yet he is not willing to accept another similar mission, having a hazy notion of honour that he cannot quite articulate, but feeling that he would rather risk the injuries and danger of scavenging than sacrifice his integrity by stealing. In this, he resembles Abdul, who, later in the text, will try to maintain a life of some honour, following what he has learned from The Master at Dongri. The two boys provide a contrast with many of the other ambitious characters – such as Asha, Fatima and Fatima's friend Cynthia – who will take any opportunity to survive and profit in Annawadi, and are less troubled by the ethical aspects of thriving in a corrupt society, culture and community.

This chapter also contains the first mention of the signs that give the text its title: advertisements for Italianate tiling, with the slogan 'Beautiful Forever' running along the wall beside Airport Road.

Key vocabulary

Eraz-ex: a stationery product resembling Wite-Out, sniffed as a drug in the slums. It is also used as a salve, to rub on wounds from barbed wire.

Q How is Sunil presented differently from the characters who do not share his moral qualms about stealing to keep one's head above water in a corrupt society?

Chapter 4: Manju (pp.50–68)

Summary: *Asha summons people to the temple to pay tribute to the Corporator, but he doesn't turn up; a eunuch dances in the temple instead; Manju teaches her students.*

Although the chapter is titled 'Manju', it begins with an emphasis instead on her mother, Asha. This title creates a structural link (connecting it with Chapter 2 and therefore ensuring a smooth narrative flow) and also reminds us that the position of a young woman such as Manju in the slum is heavily dependent on others – even though she is intellectually ambitious and driven.

Manju's story is paired with an unlikely narrative parallel: William Congreve's play *The Way of the World*, of which she is memorising summaries for school. Boo uses Congreve's themes and plot to help develop Manju's character and analyse some of the ideas of the book. Manju, for example, judges the heroine of the play because she refuses to take advantage of her own financial independence – something Manju longs for. The chapter demonstrates Manju's willingness to work for her escape from Annawadi: she studies hard, diligently teaches her students (despite lacking any qualification or experience) and does her household duties as expected.

Key point

There are 'three main ways out of poverty', according to this chapter: entrepreneurial enterprise, education and political corruption (p.62). However, the text shows that these alone are not enough; luck is also required. It doesn't matter how hard an individual works at any of these areas, they must also have good fortune.

The chapter shows how closely linked the ideas of religion, corruption, superstition and power are in Annawadians' lives. They are willing (if reluctant) to attend the temple for the Corporator, because although they know him to be part of the deeply corrupted political system, they still feel he is the only one who pays them any attention: he has provided facilities in the slum and at least pretends that Annawadians matter. When he does not arrive, they turn their fickle loyalties to the mysterious eunuch, begging for knowledge from 'the goddess lodged in the eunuch's soul' (p.55), thinking 'the goddess might know even more than Corporator Subhash Sawant' (p.56); they are willing to throw themselves on the mercy of anyone who might have more power and knowledge than they do.

Key vocabulary

Eunuch (or hijra): A castrated male or transgender (male-to-female) individual; in India they are often stigmatised socially and culturally, though can also hold some power due to superstition, as Boo illustrates.

PART TWO: THE BUSINESS OF BURNING

Chapter 5: Ghost House (pp.71–83)

Summary: *The monsoon season begins; Kehkashan leaves her husband and returns home; Karam returns from hospital; Karam agrees to spend money on improving the Annawadi hut.*

In this short chapter, Boo offers more glimpses of the challenges facing those living in extreme poverty in slums such as Annawadi – for example, the monsoon season makes already miserable living conditions seem almost unbearable. Similarly, the discussion of children being 'done away with' (p.76) is a reminder that many families cannot afford medicine or treatment for ill family members, nor the expense of raising girls, who will not be able to earn income and who will cost the family when it comes time for marriage. In India, a bride's family was traditionally obliged to provide a dowry to the groom's family; although this is now forbidden by law, it is still common practice.

In contrast to the horrors of slum life, the image of Vasai is introduced again, this time in more detail, and presented as an idyllic, spacious, healthy environment when compared to the slum. However, this aspiration has begun to feel unrealistic: 'Zehrunisa felt it premature to invest their dreams for their children in a part-owned bit of dirt that lacked even four bamboo poles and a tarp under which to sleep' (p.80). For her, the dream of escape from Annawadi feels too risky, too unreal (the 'ghost house' of the chapter title could never house her large family), and also perhaps too much a return to the restrictions of purdah.

As the chapter concludes, Boo states that the Husains' decision to improve their hut sets 'into motion the chain of contingency that would damage two families forever' (p.83). This is a rare intrusion of the narrative voice into the text. Although there is still no use of first-person from Boo's perspective as observer, here she demonstrates her omniscience (knowledge of all the events and characters' experiences) by taking a step back from the story and commenting on the plot: the characters do not know it, but we know that their lives are about to change significantly as a result of one decision.

Q The complex relationship between Fatima and Zehrunisa is developed in this chapter (especially p.77). How does Boo convey differences and similarities between them?

Chapter 6: The Hole She Called a Window (pp.84–98)

Summary: *The Husains begin the renovation; Fatima objects, fights with Zehrunisa and goes to the police to accuse her; Fatima sets herself alight.*

The way the text portrays the conflict in this scene is significant. Although Boo is careful not to apportion blame in the fight between Fatima and Zehrunisa – the two women 'started shoving each other', with neither identified as responsible for starting it (p.88) – the audience is positioned to empathise more with Zehrunisa than with Fatima. Some of the ways that Boo achieves this include:

- the language used to describe their behaviour – Fatima's initial comments are 'yelled', while Zehrunisa 'called back', implying irrational behaviour from Fatima with a calm response from Zehrunisa (p.87)
- the characters' language – Fatima calls the Husains 'bastards' (p.88), swears at them and threatens them (p.89, p.93), while Zehrunisa uses reason to argue that they built the shared wall at no cost to Fatima, and thus should be allowed occasional modifications to it
- characters' actions following the fight – Fatima is portrayed as running to the police almost like a childish tattletale about 'some small thing' (p.91), while Zehrunisa must run after her in order to preserve the Husains' side of the story
- the immediate outcomes of the fight – Zehrunisa, already put 'in a trap' by Fatima (p.89), is now effectively blackmailed by both Asha and Thokale, the police officer, for some of her family's income, while Fatima goes home and dances.

Key point

Note that although Boo presents Zehrunisa more empathetically than Fatima, she still ensures that both characters are complex. For example, while in the police station, 'Fatima was crying, so Zehrunisa turned on her own waterworks' (p.90). This brings balance to the characters, showing that Zehrunisa can also be manipulative, and that there is a possibility that Fatima is genuinely suffering, not simply trying to destroy the Husains.

This chapter also expands on the idea of corruption, as Boo details the unequal treatment that Fatima and Zehrunisa receive in the police station, based on their relative wealth.

Q Why do you think Boo has chosen this title for the chapter?

Chapter 7: The Come-Apart (pp.99–116)

Summary: *Fatima makes a new police statement in hospital; Asha attempts to mediate the conflict; Abdul and Karam are beaten in jail; Fatima dies.*

Asha's attempted intervention in the Fatima/Husain conflict while Fatima lies in Cooper Hospital demonstrates the extent to which a police case will cause trouble not just for the two families and for Asha, but also for the community in general. Although Asha's proposed solution seems reasonable, she does still intend to take a percentage of the bribe, reiterating the central role of corruption in all dealings.

There is irony in the fact that the police will intervene when an Annawadi resident is accused of a crime (largely because they expect to be able to extract blackmail money through it), yet they will do nothing to aid the everyday struggles of all the slum-dwellers. Instead, they increase the misery and difficulty with practices such as blackmailing any family who make some money.

Further corruption is evident when Poornima Paikrao influences Fatima's statement in order to help convict the Husains of a crime they have not committed, and when she accepts the new statement despite the fact that Fatima cannot read it or sign her name in order to verify its accuracy. (In the next chapter, she also pushes Zehrunisa to pay her a bribe to influence the statements she will report.)

Again, Boo complicates the text by showing how, from the police perspective, the Husains may realistically be responsible for Fatima's actions, under the British-constructed law that declares it criminal to incite a person to attempt suicide (pp.101–2). In this context, the Husains' actions and words can be taken as propelling Fatima to her immolation

– though the narrative is careful to illuminate Fatima's decisions and motivations, so that we know she is taking advantage of circumstances rather than telling the truth.

Chapter 8: The Master (pp.117–32)

Summary: *Zehrunisa tries to beg bribe money to get her family out of jail; she succeeds in having Abdul recorded as a juvenile; he goes to the Dongri juvenile detention centre, where he meets The Master.*

As their money dwindles and she has no means to rescue her husband and children from detention, Zehrunisa becomes desperate, making mistakes such as telling people about Thokale's bribe money. Yet even as her distress increases, she retains a focus on her children: particularly Abdul, for whom she manages to secure false papers, hoping that he will be tried as a juvenile instead of as an adult.

In Dongri, Abdul experiences a kind of life he has never seen before, including bathing daily, sharing conversation with others and not having to work all day – and in this change of lifestyle, he feels 'something had happened to his heart' (p.129) and he experiences emotions, such as empathy, for which he never really had time or energy in his hardworking life in Annawadi. On the other hand, he also recognises that his ability to earn money sorting garbage, without having to resort to criminal activity, constitutes a kind of freedom that other children have never had. Similarly, the food in Dongri is terrible compared to what Zehrunisa offers her family. Even the police and the guards at Dongri suffer from some of the health problems Abdul is familiar with from the slums.

So for Abdul, the prison is both more and less of a trial than his slum life. In other ways, too, it is exactly the same. Corruption here, for example, is rife, just like at home – as seen when a bribe is demanded to record his official age as seventeen rather than twenty-one. However, by some fortune, this demand is withdrawn and the 'friendly doctor' (p.130) ends up declaring Abdul to be seventeen even though he has no funds to pay the bribe.

Abdul's most significant experience in Dongri is meeting The Master: a teacher with the charisma of a cult leader. Abdul has not come across such a person before, and is entranced by The Master's demonstrative, emotional, preacher-like teachings; by his moral positions; and by the 'virtuous path' (p.132) that becomes a new possible life path for Abdul.

Q Why do you think The Master appeals to Abdul in such a powerful way?

Q Zehrunisa feels that 'every choice she'd made thus far' since the burning has been 'wrong' (p.121). Do you agree? Why or why not?

PART THREE: A LITTLE WILDNESS

Chapter 9: Marquee Effect (pp.135–51)

Summary: *Asha and her family visit Vidarbha; Asha and Manju search for a groom for Manju; Asha leaves a family celebration of her fortieth birthday to answer the call of a policeman with whom she will have sex.*

Two central ideas in this chapter are a world that contrasts with Annawadi (the traditional farming lands of Asha and Mahadeo's families and the Kunbis farming caste) and Manju's role as a marketable, marriageable young woman. The portrayal of rural Maharashtra as even more miserable than the slums is linked to the inevitability of Manju's eventual marriage, when she observes that if her mother arranges a marriage for her in Vidarbha, 'she would run away' (p.141) – such is the poverty and struggle in the rural agricultural life. In rural India, the farming practices have become unsustainable; rich politicians own and run the land, taking advantage of workers; and the suicide rates are immeasurably high (p.137). Just like in Annawadi, survival is a struggle.

For Manju, the struggle now includes seeking a profitable marriage as well as continuing to carry the household domestic load and teaching her students. She turns her energy to finding a husband as diligently as she works at the other areas in her life: she joins groups and does her best to widen her social circles, and is realistic about who she might meet, knowing that Vijay – a fellow student she likes – could never tolerate her low status.

Q Which lifestyle do you consider more difficult: slum life or rural life? What evidence in the text supports your opinion?

Chapter 10: Parrots, Caught and Sold (pp.152–65)

Summary: *A scavenger dies on the road, followed by a number of other deaths around Annawadi; Sunil and Sonu scavenge together; Abdul is sent home from Dongri until his trial; Kalu dies.*

Death begins and ends the chapter: first the death of an 'unidentified' scavenger (the official police position only; some Annawadians know who he is) and then the death of Kalu, the closest thing Abdul has to a friend. In between, a relentless parade of corpses streams through the chapter, emphasising a number of central ideas in the text, such as:

- the risks, dangers and harsh nature of extreme poverty – death is never far away from anyone's reality
- the loneliness of slum life – though many people pass the first dying scavenger, nobody has time, energy or confidence to help him
- corruption – the various corpses are unidentified and un-autopsied, because this remains the most profitable option for the police
- the role of fate – the only real difference between those who die and those who survive in this chapter is sheer luck.

Abdul returns home from Dongri, and while this seems to be an event of central importance, it is sidelined, leaving space for the chapter to focus on the deaths that occur. Other important ideas and motifs touched upon include the resourcefulness of young men such as Sunil, Sonu and Kalu; the importance of allegiances and relationships, however tenuous (such as that between Sunil and Sonu); the ever-present risk of slum destruction; and the role of superstition in Annawadians' lives – many think that the deaths in this chapter are the result of a curse left by Fatima.

Q Other than the slum parrots mentioned in the text (p.159), to what might the title of Chapter 10 refer?

Chapter 11: Proper Sleep (pp.166–74)

Summary: *Kalu's death is misreported; Sanjay, a witness, is threatened by the police and commits suicide; Sunil and Abdul become closer; everyone is afraid to tell Sanjay's mother the truth about how he died.*

The tone initiated in the previous chapter is continued: death is again a recurring motif (alluded to, symbolically, in the chapter title, since death may be the only 'proper sleep' many of the characters ever have), as is the fact that not only the deaths but also the reactions to them are completely out of Annawadians' control. As in life, the slum residents are at the mercy of the harsh realities of poverty and the equally harsh realities of power and corruption – the deaths do not matter to those in control, and so they are misreported or even hidden in the interests of making the police look better.

This short chapter also emphasises the contrasts of Annawadi, including those between:

- the official and the actual – the numbers of murders reported in Sahar district compared to the number that occur; Kalu's and Sanjay's reported versus actual causes of and motivations for death
- wealth and poverty – the 'Beautiful Forever' tiles advertisement and the 'We Care' sign, compared with Sunil feeling 'small and sad and useless' (p.168).

Q Describe the language Boo uses in the final paragraph of this chapter. How does this contribute to your understanding of the themes of the text?

Q What hints does Boo provide, before Sanjay's suicide, of his impending death? Does this make the death more shocking to you, or less? Why?

PART FOUR: UP AND OUT

Chapter 12: Nine Nights of Dance (pp.177–89)

Summary: *Annawadi prepares for the Navratri festival; Meena consumes rat poison and dies six days later.*

In the depths of extreme poverty, there are still times for dancing and fairy lights – 'exuberant distraction' from the pain and difficulties of slum life (p.181). However, even this joyous occasion is marred by horror and desperation: Meena's final suicide attempt coincides with the first night of Navratri, and by two-thirds of the way into the festival she has died in hospital, ending the celebrations for that year.

Key point

Note the contrast between the emotional tone of this chapter – desperation, sorrow, hopelessness – and the section title, 'Up and Out'. Boo offers an inspiring optimism with the title, but quickly dashes it, just as many hopes and efforts are dashed in Annawadi.

Meena's suicide, described as 'one decision about her life she got to make' (p.188), is a clear attempt to escape slum life and her future as a young village bride: though death may not seem preferable to even the grimmest existence, for a girl such as Meena, who has no skills, no agency and no hope of changing her circumstances, it feels the best option.

Chapter 13: Something Shining (pp.190–9)

Summary: *Muslim terrorists attack hotels in Mumbai; Sunil becomes a thief.*

In Annawadi, the impacts of the terrorism are both immediate and prolonged: scavenging is impossible near the airport due to increased security, and in the longer term, the attacks discourage tourism, meaning the nearby airport and hotels are no longer profitable sources for the various slum-dwelling entrepreneurs. The global market, too, is still struggling (the Tamil game-shed owner offers a simplified explanation at the opening of the chapter). So a life that was already difficult for Annawadians becomes even harder.

Boo conveys these changes through one of the secondary characters, Sunil, who is forced into thieving, as his scavenging no longer supports him. With this comes a change to his confidence, as he starts to doubt his place in the world. Stealing scrap metal from the airport carries high risk, but also brings a powerful experience of elation: when he looks down from the roof of the half-built car park, he is in an open space that no other part of Annawadi or Mumbai can offer, and can look down at the world and the people below, feeling connected to them from his safe distance.

Q How does the focus on a single character in this chapter help develop the themes of the text?

Chapter 14: The Trial (pp.200–12)

Summary: *Karam and Kehkashan's Fast-Track trial begins; Paikrao blackmails them; witnesses, including Fatima's husband and Cynthia, give evidence.*

The corruption in the Indian court system – despite Karam's deep faith in the judiciary – is revealed in a number of ways in this chapter. Not all individuals are motivated by malicious intent but, rather, are shown to be the product of a deeply dysfunctional system. For example, the overburdened judge for the Fast-Track Sessions Court cannot spare the time while her incompetent stenographer translates slowly, so instead the judge simplifies and distils witness testimonies. This removes complexities and, likely, introduces inaccuracies in testimony; however, the judge's motivation is not to influence the trial one way or the other (though this is a probable outcome), but rather to rush through the case – merely one of dozens of concurrent cases for her. Ultimately, this actually benefits the Husains, when Cynthia's slightly muddled testimony goes down on record as far less damning evidence than she intended.

Other examples of corruption in this chapter include:

- the selective choice of Annawadian witnesses (many who were not even present during the events in question)
- Poornima Paikrao's attempt at extorting the Husains (pp.203–4)
- Cynthia's prior attempt to blackmail the Husains (p.210).

The prevalence of corruption in this facet of Indian undercity life, as in so many others, supports the text's suggestion that poverty is associated with a lack of agency.

Q Who is most affected by corruption in this chapter? What does this tell you about the values the text endorses?

Chapter 15: Ice (pp.213–20)

Summary: *The Husains struggle to maintain an income; the impact of the terrorism continues to damage the Indian economy (including as it relates to Annawadians); the Husains again resist attempts at extortion regarding the trial outcome; a new judge is assigned to their case.*

This chapter parallels the progress of the Husains' trials with the trial of Ajmal Kasab, the only surviving perpetrator of the recent terror attacks. Though Abdul knows that Kasab's punishment (both official and unofficial) will be horrific, Abdul still envies him, because the punishment is perceived to be earned. To envy such treatment shows the extent of pain Abdul is experiencing due to the lack of justice in the system when it comes to his own case: he believes the extreme violence Kasab is likely to suffer is at least 'less stressful than being beaten when you were innocent' (p.216).

Though the family business has all but disintegrated, some positives are linked to this. For example, Mirchi has matured and accepted responsibility for contributing to his family's wellbeing, even finding some of his long-hoped-for hotel work in the process. Abdul, meanwhile, achieves a small sense of perspective and even relief from his situation, spending time in Saki Naka and seeing that there may still be a world for him beyond the trial.

Q Abdul thinks he is 'probably little different' from the 'cynical, corrupt people around him' (p.218). What evidence in the text supports this?

Chapter 16: Black and White (pp.221–32)

Summary: *Asha becomes depressed; the governmental plans to reclaim the airport slumlands progress as the election looms; Asha finds a new scheme for money and power and gives up her slumlord dream.*

In contrast to Abdul's tentative positivity in Saki Naka (though it is certainly tempered by his realisation at Haji Ali), Chapter 16 opens with the despairing tones of Asha, who, despite her constant efforts, is finding her slumlording life 'tedious' and unrewarding (p.222). All her plans for getting away from poverty are 'schemes that had sucked up months before sputtering out' (p.222), and 'something bright in her had been eclipsed' (p.223).

Key point

The poem Asha recites (p.222) sums up many of the slum-dwellers' experiences of life: unrewarding struggles followed by unexpected deaths.

It is not only Asha's confidence but also the community's respect for her that dwindles in this chapter, as summarised by a Tamil woman's assertion: 'always she was sly, but now we know there is no one she won't hurt for money' (p.226). Her ambition has taken her to new depths rather than the heights she once hoped for, yet again emphasising the idea that agency is a very rare commodity in Annawadi, since even those who try to escape their fates are ultimately punished.

As the election preparations ramp up, in the slums as in the rest of India, they focus attention on many ongoing ideas in the text, including:

- the nature of corruption in the Indian system – it is not always secretive but often blatant, as with the sewer covers (p.230)

- the sense that voting is empowering, despite the corruption – the eunuchs are desperate to vote even though they do not have any real political preference, since no party is likely to enact meaningful change in their lives (p.230)
- the pressure on those with any power – such as Asha, not only to help the Corporator through her influence in Annawadi, but also to do so no matter which party is represented (p.222)
- the persistence of the slum-dwellers, as represented by 'the new Asha', off to meet a suitor in her own choice of dress and determined – despite past disappointments – that this venture will succeed (p.232).

Q Explain what you think Boo means by the sentence: 'Gold pots flaked away, revealing mud pots' (p.221). How does this image relate to the rest of the text?

Chapter 17: A School, a Hospital, a Cricket Field (pp.233–44)

Summary: *The airport begins the slum demolishment; Kehkashan and Karam are declared not guilty; Abdul's trial is put off for more than a year; the Vasai plot has been sold; Sunil returns to scavenging.*

The final chapter opens with the beginning of the end for Annawadi itself as the 'Beautiful Forever' wall – an emblem of hope throughout the text – is torn down. Yet even in this destruction, some of the most irrepressible spirits of the slum, the children, find optimism as they watch the bulldozers unearth 'salable commodities' (p.234). This reminds us that in a life of poverty, hope and despair are almost inseparable. The image of hope is enhanced by the symbolism of the younger Husains observing the development together with Fatima's daughters, unhindered by the conflict that has all but destroyed their families' lives. Fatima's daughter Heena's successful rescue of a piece of 'treasure' (p.235) completes the portrait of optimism.

This optimism is contrasted with the hopelessness of the Husains' new subsistence living, and Kehkashan's sense of futility at even engaging in their own case any longer. In the courtroom, her religion and culture are devalued, as the judge jokes about her burqa and gives information in English (p.238). As they await the verdict outside, a dog dies in the street, symbolising the disposable nature of their existence. It is a surprise to readers, then, as much as to the Husains when they are unceremoniously declared not guilty: yet further evidence suggesting that the fates of the slum-dwellers are near arbitrary, and always in the hands of those wealthier and more powerful.

Abdul is less fortunate. Nothing – from his mother's praying to pressure from Poornima Paikrao to a police officer's threats at Dongri – speeds up his case, and for over a year he waits in painful uncertainty: 'a suspended state between guilt and innocence' (p.240) that he believes will continue forever. The 'ice' he wanted to become is melting under pressure, and Abdul no longer has optimism that he can become better than what he is made from and surrounded by. He finds small comfort in 'master[ing] a few feet of gummy road' (p.242) as he tries to earn money.

The text's final image – of the miserable but profitable garbage awaiting Sunil above the river – parallels the conclusion of Abdul's narrative: Abdul's fate is as uncertain as the risk of jumping to the ledge to collect the trash. Only a small amount of effort and skill, and a large quantity of luck, can make the difference between survival and death.

Author's Note (pp.247–54)

Summary: *Boo explains why and how she researched and wrote the book, including postulating theories to explain some of what she saw.*

Although not part of the narrative proper, the Author's Note contributes information and context. Here, Boo enters her own text as a character, part of the story of Annawadi. The Note provides a structural parallel for the Prologue, so that the two sections 'bookend' the main narrative. Boo concludes with a philosophical question to readers, encouraging them to engage with the narrative and interrogate her conclusions as well as their own belief systems.

Q Why do you think Boo includes this note?

CHARACTERS & RELATIONSHIPS

Abdul Hakim Husain

Key quotes

'*Avoid trouble*. This was the operating principle of Abdul Hakim Husain, an idea so fiercely held that it seemed imprinted on his physical form. He had deep-set eyes and sunken cheeks, a body work-hunched and wiry …' (p.xi)

'Abdul didn't talk much, and when he did, it was as if he'd spent weeks privately working over some little idea.' (p.10)

'… Abdul was as cautious about marrying as he was about everything else.' (p.78)

'He was a categorizer of people as well as of garbage …' (p.88)

Abdul is the central character in the narrative; although there are other characters whose perspectives are almost as prominent (including Asha, Manju and Sunil), it is his story that runs most strongly through the text. Boo emphasises this structurally by beginning and ending the text with scenes from his life.

Although his parents gave him 'a peaceful name … Abdul Hakim, a person who cures others just by his own understanding' (p.122), Abdul's experience in Annawadi is far from peaceful. He labours hard to support his large family (even late in the text, when business has become extremely unprofitable) and is unfairly accused of causing Fatima's death. His mother sees 'so much turmoil inside him – I don't think he's been happy for a single day in Annawadi' (p.79).

Limitations

While Abdul is responsible for supporting his family, he is only a young man – 'sixteen years old, or maybe nineteen – his parents were hopeless with dates' (p.ix) – and not a particularly imaginative or bright one at that. Nor is he as brave as he likes to imagine – not even as brave as his little brother Mirchi – though he considers such attentiveness to potential danger an asset rather than a downfall (p.xx). Descriptions of him often do not portray him in a very flattering light:

- In the opening pages he becomes 'mule-brained with panic' (p.ix) and lacks inspiration to run away properly, returning home immediately.
- Words are, for him, 'stiff and slow'; his father observes that Abdul 'didn't have the mind for school' (p.xiii).
- Abdul himself says 'it takes me longer than other people to understand things' (p.126).

Abdul has only one 'sort-of-friend' (p.12) and is otherwise fairly solitary, though he is able to form strong working relationships, such as with Sunil. He has never experienced love, except as a deep affection for his littlest brother, and is somewhat unsettled by this, worrying that he is missing an essential element of life. Though he is engaged to a girl in Saki Naka, the neighbouring slum, this is not a significant relationship in the text, and indeed is terminated by the girl's family when Abdul is in jail (p.119).

Strengths and transition

While his intellectual confidence and capacities may be lacking, Abdul's vocational abilities abound. He is physically 'agile' (p.xiii), an extremely fast and successful garbage sorter. He is determined and hardworking, and has embraced the role of provider for his family; his father cannot work due to persistent illness, so the family depends on him (with the help of Zehrunisa's business acumen and assertiveness). Abdul doesn't want his younger brother to have to do the same work, knowing Mirchi hates it; instead, he compassionately wishes 'something better' for him (p.163).

Key point

Abdul thinks hard about the world around him, forming and modifying his own system of moral and ethical behaviour. He has goals, even if small and simple, and he understands the political and social dynamics of the slum more clearly than might be expected of him, given his lack of education.

Abdul's most significant relationship in the text is with The Master, in the Dongri juvenile detention centre. The Master is a teacher who inspires Abdul, profoundly changing his perspective on the world and awakening in him a passionate desire to be morally commendable. While the accusations against Abdul and the taxing requirements that he travel to Dongri three times a week (almost destroying his business abilities) are key crisis points for him, it is as a result that he meets The Master, and this interaction is a turning point. For Abdul, 'The Master's words lit up a virtuous path' (pp.131–2); he had never before seen an alternative available to him, and from this point onward he vows to be 'better and more honourable', even though he has already been 'virtuous in some ways' (p.132), considering the behaviour of his peers. He maintains these commitments with integrity and, though they bring him little reward financially or in terms of the outcome of his trial, they furnish him with an internal strength. While Boo shows that his circumstances defeat his desires to be 'better than what he was made of' (p.218), the text still argues that these values are admirable in a world of poverty and corruption.

Karam Husain

Key quotes

'Abdul didn't dare voice the great flaw of his father, Karam Husain: too sick to sort much garbage, not sick enough to stay off his wife.' (p.xv)

'Karam ... sought to keep his children incurious about aspects of Indian life beyond their control.' (p.32)

Father to nine surviving children, Karam suffers from tuberculosis and is unable to provide for his large family. He is portrayed as kindly but ineffectual, in contrast to those characters who achieve things through their lack of compassion for others (such as Asha or the corrupt politicians). Despite being a secondary figure in his children's lives compared to Zehrunisa, Karam is still someone Abdul respects; when they are in prison, Abdul would 'rather be beaten' (p.107) than see Karam beaten.

Another area in which Karam is unsuccessful is securing a plot of land where he might breathe cleaner air and his family have a better life; he sees Vasai as 'the ideal village-city hybrid: a place where opportunity and parental respect weren't mutually exclusive' (p.80), and he hopes to pay off their investment and move the family there. Though he dreams of Vasai, Karam is not supportive of others' dreams – he criticises Asha, calling her 'mad in her ambitions' (p.85). As it turns out, his own dreams amount to nothing, as he loses the deposit on the land when it is sold to another family.

A key moment for Karam is in Chapter 15, when his reading of Urdu newspapers is shown to at last benefit him and his family, allowing him to safely resist the exorbitant blackmail Poornima Paikrao and Fatima's husband attempt to force upon him. This is described as a 'small triumph of information over corruption' (p.219), and suggests that education is an important value in the text. While Karam has been unable to support his family through physical labour, in this instance his ability to read Urdu and his insistence on researching as much as possible before the case affords him some agency over his own and his family's fate.

Zehrunisa Husain

Key quotes

'... Abdul believed his mother, Zehrunisa, to be right about most things. She was tender and playful with her children, and her only great flaw, in the opinion of Abdul ... was the language she used when haggling.' (p.xv)

' ... a woman who'd been raised in some nowhere of a village to be burqa-clad, devout.' (p.xv)

'It was her habit to exaggerate her poverty ...' (p.40)

Zehrunisa, mother of Abdul and his eight siblings, is from an impoverished background in Pakistan, and was wedded in an arranged marriage with Karam. Though they seem to have a relatively peaceful relationship – particularly compared with many other marriages portrayed in Annawadi, where domestic violence is not uncommon – they disagree on many things, from fundamental beliefs and values to decisions about their future. For example, Zehrunisa does not share Karam's passion for the Vasai plot, and it is at her insistence that Karam agrees to spend money on their new kitchen (inadvertently setting in motion the events leading to Fatima's burning). Indeed, she holds much power in their relationship; as her daughter observes, Zehrunisa is 'where the family authority resided in a crisis' (p.94). Such responsibility was at first forced upon her, due to Karam's illness, but she has come to embrace it, to the extent that she resents the idea of potentially returning to the restriction of purdah in Vasai.

Key point

Zehrunisa's changing attitudes to purdah reflect a key idea in the text: that often one cannot control one's circumstances, only adapt to them. At first Zehrunisa hates having to go out and work with the men, terrified to be alone out of the house, but she comes to value this freedom.

Though Zehrunisa cannot read, her lack of education is not presented as a failing, and she is portrayed as strong in many other ways. For example, she takes motherhood very seriously, pandering to Lallu, her youngest, and sacrificing herself to care for the others. She is very proud of her children's health (p.81) and suffers greatly when Kehkashan is arrested: for her, 'seeing her gentle daughter escorted by officers into jail' is the 'end of the world' (p.120). As a wife, too, Zehrunisa is loyal, doing her best to get her sick husband out of jail. However, she refuses to be blackmailed into paying Asha to make the case disappear, leading Asha to conclude that Zehrunisa 'doesn't understand the basic thing: You pay early, it costs less later on' (p.97).

Mirchi Husain

Key quotes

'The younger Husain boy didn't know the value of anything, and when Sunil and the other waste-pickers tried to help him, he made fun of their boils.' (p.118)

'... the family catastrophe had changed him. He'd become a fast, competent garbage sorter and taken every other job he could find.' (p.214)

Mirchi is not interested in the garbage-sorting business and openly judges his older brother for the work he undertakes, even though it is what funds their family and his (as it turns out, failed) studies. He has aspirations to something better, something cleaner, something easier – such as the hotel work some of the Annawadi boys manage to gain.

In the later chapters, however, Mirchi rises to the challenge of helping support the family when Abdul can no longer work full-time and the price of garbage has dropped dramatically. His new hardworking philosophy shows how 'the family catastrophe had changed him' (p.214), supporting the text's idea that growth can come from tragedy.

Kehkashan Husain

Key quotes

'To her younger brothers and sisters, Kehkashan had been a second mother – a more organized, less exhausted version of the original.' (p.74)

'Atahar said he didn't mind quitting school to help his family, but Kehkashan minded, very much.' (p.238)

Kehkashan is not as well developed a character in the text as Abdul or her parents – as evidenced by the fact that after the Prologue, she is not mentioned until she returns home to Annawadi from her failed marriage in Chapter 5. She does not have a chapter dedicated to her narrative point of view, as many other characters do; however, Boo conveys important aspects of her character through key incidents, such as when she makes the difficult decision to leave her unfaithful husband, demonstrating that she has confidence and trusts her own ethical values. She also takes charge of the family in crisis, directing her father and brothers to run away from Fatima, showing that she has presence of mind even in distress. Finally, she lies when Zehrunisa comes to visit her in prison, saying that she is 'fine' (p.119), showing a desire to protect her mother's feelings.

Fatima ('The One Leg') Shaikh

Key quotes

'Had she been another sort of woman, her affairs might have been a scandal; that she was disabled made them a joke.' (p.71)

'... Fatima thought wretched early years should be rounded out by a few good ones, which she had yet to have.' (p.72)

'She has a crack in her – she's cracked ...' (Abdul, p.89)

Fatima (named Sita but renamed by her husband) feels her disability keenly. She is happiest in the afternoons – 'husband at work, daughters at school' (p.73) – when her missing leg doesn't impede her sexually; she has affairs with men, feeling useful and appreciated in a way she cannot on her crutches while trying to parent her daughters and survive the slum. She is less angry about her missing leg than about others' treatment of her because of it: she wants 'recognition that she was as human as anyone else' (p.72).

Fatima is portrayed as a morally dubious character (positioning readers to empathise with the Husains in the court case). As well as her many affairs, her abilities as a mother are questioned: not only is she presented as physically unable to care adequately for her 'needy, rambunctious' daughters Heena and Noori (p.73), whom she has been known to abuse (pp.75–6), but there is also the question of her sickly young daughter Medina, who drowned in a bucket – an accident many quietly suspect Fatima of being responsible for. She is violent with neighbours she dislikes, using her crutches as a weapon. On the other hand, Boo is careful to contextualise Fatima's failings: not only has she faced the lifelong hardship of disability but she has also suffered the indignities and unhappiness of her arranged marriage to Mahadeo, an older, poor man, who is Muslim when she was raised Hindu.

After setting herself on fire, Fatima tells so many versions of her story that eventually she becomes 'confused herself' as to the truth (p.104) – though it is possible this confusion is caused by the infection that eventually claims her life. Her desperation to incriminate the Husains is presented as being out of proportion to the actual harm they did her (by damaging the shared wall and trading insults).

Asha Waghekar

Key quotes

'… a fighter-cock of a woman who … longed to be Annawadi's first female slumlord, then ride the city's inexorable corruption into the middle class.' (p.xvii)

'Asha had always been more practical than ideological …' (p.22)

'… little happened in Annawadi that didn't get back to her eventually.' (p.26)

Asha, a thirty-nine-year-old 'kindergarten teacher with mysterious connections to local politicians and the police' (pp.7–8), is one of the few Annawadians who manage to secure any form of power for themselves. An active member of the political party Shiv Sena – composed largely of Mumbai Hindus who blame interstate migrants for overcrowding in the city (the party's founder modelled some of his views on Hitler's, p.12) – Asha is loyal to the local Corporator, who is also a Shiv Sena member. She relies on him for her campaign to become slumlord and he, in turn, relies on her influence in Annawadi for his own purposes.

Asha, although married, has a level of independence unusual for a woman in Annawadi. Like Zehrunisa, this is because of her husband – in Asha's case, her husband is a hopeless drunk, so she has more or less raised their three children on her own: 'had the situation been otherwise, she might not have come to know her own brain' (p.18). Her circumstances, which could have been a curse, in fact allow her to pursue her political interests and also several affairs, often related to the politics of gaining power in the slum.

Asha thinks of herself as religious, but her experience shows that her prayers and her fortunes do not seem to be linked, so she doesn't practise faithfully – she seems blessed, and gets what she wants much of the time anyway. This is true despite, in the later chapters, a string of disappointments and failures. By the conclusion of the text she is again in a position of power and financial stability as she engages in the corrupt scheme purporting to bring education to all Indian children.

Manju Waghekar

Key quotes

'... Manju was nicer than she had to be, given her looks, her mother's political connections, and her punishing schedule.' (p.57)

'... the most-everything girl ...' (p.110)

'Manju's hopes pressed against her well-honed tendency toward realism ...' (p.149)

The 'magnificent nineteen-year-old-daughter' of Asha (p.21), Manju is obedient, beautiful and clever (the only girl at college in the slum): all qualities of which her mother is proud. But she is sentimental, which Asha considers a failing and blames herself for (p.27). This is echoed in the Husain family, where Zehrunisa despairs over her son Safdar, who is 'dreamy and impractical, like her husband' (p.85) – pragmatism is valued in the slums. However, Manju is pragmatic in a number of other ways. She runs the school her mother is responsible for, often using it as an opportunity to further her own studies while showing genuine care for her young students.

Her most significant relationships are with her mother and her friend Meena. Manju is dutiful and respectful towards her mother, yet not submissive. She is portrayed as being strong and intelligent, just like Asha. Manju, however, shows far more compassion and kindness than her mother. It is possible that her youth is responsible for this difference:

she has yet to become jaded by the world. But the weight of responsibility placed upon her (she must do all the housework as well as teaching the students and studying; she will also be expected to marry as her mother decides) suggests that if she were to become cynical, this would already have happened. Rather, she has a slightly gentler personality than her mother. This compassion and kindness come to light in her friendship with Meena, where the girls share a mutually supportive relationship. (See further discussion under 'Alliance' in the 'Themes, Ideas and Values' section.)

Sunil Sharma

Key quotes

'Sunil was a seed of a boy, smaller even than Abdul, but he considered himself more sophisticated than the other scavengers.' (p.33)

'Sunil rarely got angry when he discovered the secret reasons behind the ways people behaved. Having a sense of the way the world operated, beyond its pretenses, seemed to him an armoring thing.' (p.33)

Sunil is embarrassed by his father and was more comfortable living in the children's home, where he was wise to the corruption of the place, and where he appreciated the skills he learned, such as reading and some basic maths and geography. He has always looked out for his little sister, since their father does not.

Sunil is bright and proud and prefers dignity to begging, though his dreams of being chosen for a new home at the orphanage due to his dignity were just that – dreams – and he soon recognised them for the fantasy they were. Instead, he is practical and finds ways to survive slum life.

After the terror attacks and subsequent economic collapse, Sunil loses confidence as well as profitable work, and is forced to turn to stealing, a decision with which he feels uncomfortable: 'every month that passed, he felt less sure of where he belonged among the human traffic in the city below. Once, he had believed he was smart and might become something' (p.197). Yet with a sense of persistence common to many

Annawadians, he eventually returns to scavenging, and even holds some optimism of starting a new life 'somewhere outside the city, where there were trees and flowers' (p.243).

Kalu

Key quotes

> 'To Annawadi boys, Kalu had been a star. To the authorities of the overcity, he was a nuisance case to be dispensed with.' (p.168)

Fifteen-year-old Kalu steals recyclables from bins at the airport, and is 'the closest thing Abdul had to a friend' (p.44). He is even welcomed by Zehrunisa, who often feeds him, and whom he begins to call 'amma' (mother), as he lacks a connection with his own father and brothers. He is also kind to Sunil, occasionally giving him money for food. 'Kalu' is a nickname meaning 'black boy'; he has darker skin than some other Indians, which is usually indicative of lower status in Indian society, but Kalu is popular with other boys (not least for his entertaining impersonations of film stars and local personalities) and successful in his work. His death is dismissed by the authorities as being tuberculosis-related – though this doesn't stop the Sahar police threatening to charge some of the road boys with his murder.

Meena

Key quotes

> 'Things were inflicted upon her – regular beatings, the new engagement to marry. But what did she ever get to decide?' (p.182)

Meena is fifteen and was the first girl born in Annawadi: her parents were among the Tamil workers who built the slum on the swamp. They are from the Dalit caste, the 'untouchables'. Like Manju, Meena is expected to fulfil all housekeeping duties, but her parents and brothers do not permit her any of the independence Manju has. She is regularly beaten, is not allowed to leave the house, and is soon to be married and sent to a village; though she secretly likes a boy from a neighbouring slum who is in love with her, she knows they cannot do more than flirt.

Meena ponders Fatima's burning, thinking perhaps to 'escape the situation if you know you're going to be miserable' (p.184) is a better option than accepting an undesirable arranged marriage. However, even in such thoughts, Meena is considerate of others: she says she would use poison because loved ones' final memories are too horrible with self-immolation. Her suicide is not 'acting out of anger, as Fatima had done' (p.188). Rather, she has made several attempts before her final one in Chapter 12.

Meena's family blame Manju's 'modern influence' (p.189) for Meena's death, which is ironic, as Manju would never do such a thing against her mother's wishes or reputation: 'Meena had been the hot resister of daughterly responsibilities, not she' (p.229).

THEMES, IDEAS & VALUES

Poverty

Key quotes

'For nearly all the waking hours of nearly all the years he could remember, he'd been buying and selling to recyclers the things that richer people threw away.' (p.ix)

'To be poor in Annawadi, or in any Mumbai slum, was to be guilty of one thing or another.' (p.xviii)

'She'd known abjectness, loathed its recollection, and raised her son for a modern age of ruthless competition.' (p.111)

The impact of poverty is a central theme in *Behind the Beautiful Forevers*, one that is closely linked with other ideas and themes such as hope and corruption.

All the slum-dwellers live in extreme poverty, and any portrayals of wealth and wealthier characters are presented as a startling contrast to the experiences of Annawadians. This contrast is illustrated in the physical setting of the text, with the opulent luxury of the airport hotels literally overshadowing the 335 huts of Annawadi. Another illustration of this contrast is in the motif captured in the book's title: the signs advertising shiny new tiling, proclaiming they will remain 'beautiful forever' (p.37). These 'sunshine-yellow advertisements' (p.37) hide the slum from Airport Road and provide an incongruous boundary to the life of poverty in Annawadi. It is particularly symbolic that when the Husains attempt their kitchen renovation – the event that provokes Fatima's burning and the accusations and legal case that follow – they are aspiring to the sort of illusory and inaccessible comfort, cleanliness and happiness represented in the tiling advertisement: a lifestyle associated with those who have wealth.

Rather than offering statistical information about financial inequality, Boo demonstrates the day-to-day meaning of poverty by presenting intimate, detailed portraits of individual lives. As she observes in her

Author's Note, 'statistics about the poor sometimes have a tenuous relation to lived experience' (p.249), so Boo concentrates on the latter rather than the former. While there is some information about the remuneration for work in the case of the few lucky Annawadians who have anything approaching a regular income (at the height of the success of the family business, Abdul is earning roughly US$11 per day), the focus is more on 'showing' than 'telling': the text shows us what it actually means to live under such conditions. This links with the creative nonfiction genre: rather than providing figures or data about world poverty, Boo offers concrete examples of the reality of poverty, in a narrative context.

For example, the inventory of the Husain belongings (pp.85–6) helps put into perspective the levels of poverty in the slum. The Husains are considered very well-off by Annawadi standards, but this translates to such meagre belongings as two quilts, a cupboard, a cracked mirror, a rusty bed, a television and some kitchenware – all shared between eleven family members. This allows readers a personal, emotional connection to the issues of global financial inequality with which Boo is concerned, rather than an abstract, theoretical understanding, which can be much more distancing, particularly when it comes to large-scale social problems such as global poverty.

In *Behind the Beautiful Forevers*, Boo shows that extreme poverty dictates all aspects of life. Areas in which the text demonstrates that those in poverty are suffering include:

- access to basic resources, such as sanitation, clean water, food, shelter and health services
- political and democratic representation and input
- personal safety (including lack of security within their living environment, and extreme lack of support from law enforcement).

These areas, in turn, impact on Annawadians' ability to access further educational, social and vocational opportunities.

However, the text also argues that despite living in poverty, the characters of Annawadi strive towards fulfilment in terms of their philosophical, interpersonal and professional goals: 'even the person who lives like a dog still has a kind of life' (p.198). While poverty can restrict access to and choices about opportunities, it does not always change human motivation and behaviour. Boo encourages us not to dismiss the poor on the grounds of their financial status.

Interestingly, the terror attacks in Mumbai lead wealthy Indians to realise that 'their security could not be requisitioned privately. They were dependent on the same public safety system that ill served the poor' (p.216). This strengthens Boo's argument that wealth and poverty are circumstantial and that humans share desires, fears and behaviours regardless of their financial status. The terrorism helps those who are financially successful to see, even if temporarily, that they too can be vulnerable. This incident links closely with the theme of corruption, illustrating the level of systemic governmental dysfunction the terrorist attack highlights. In identifying the systemic nature of such corruption, Boo avoids apportioning blame to individuals. For example, police officers aren't adequately trained to do their job (such as in the use of weapons), which is presented as a reason behind their failure to respond appropriately to the attack. They are also disempowered by the system that reinforces the cycles of poverty illustrated in the text.

Hope and betterment

Key quotes

'Competence in English ... was a potential springboard out of the slums.' (p.60)

'Almost everyone here improved his hut when he was able, in pursuit of not just better hygiene and protection from the monsoon but of protection from the airport authority.' (p.86)

'Abdul had been aiming for a future like the past, but with more money.' (p.111)

'Asha believed a person seeking betterment should try as many schemes as possible, since it was hard to predict which one might work.' (p.144)

In Boo's Author's Note, she argues that 'hope is not a fiction' (p.253), and this idea is embodied by the people of Annawadi. It is hope of a better future that keeps most of the characters in *Behind the Beautiful*

Forevers continuing their difficult struggles in the slum. There are as many forms of hope, and strategies and plans towards betterment, as there are individuals in the text. Characters experience varying degrees of success in their endeavours, with many finding at least some satisfaction in the short term, while most are still destined to live extremely difficult lives of poverty despite their efforts. Boo shows that hope is an enduring human trait – since nearly every character exhibits some form of it – but that it rarely correlates with success, and even more rarely leads to any kind of permanent escape from poverty.

Education

A central value in the text, education is seen by individuals as well as by the government as a way of advancing in life, and there are widespread beliefs that children should have access to education. This value is illustrated through:

- Manju's dedication to her studies and ambition to succeed academically; this is paralleled by her commitment to teaching her students, even though she has no qualifications and little formal knowledge of how to do so
- the Department of Education plan to make education accessible to all children (pp.226–7)
- Sunil's efforts to learn to read and understand basic maths while at the orphanage
- Sonu's commitment to studying in the evenings, even though his work precludes him from attending Marol Municipal, where he is enrolled – he believes education is a key to improved employment (pp.157–8).

Despite the prevalent respect for education, however, Boo's text demonstrates that its benefits are barely accessible for the poor. The Department of Education plan is undermined by corruption from its very inception, and the education young Annawadians strive for is never shown to increase their opportunities or quality of life.

Sex

Both Fatima and Asha use sex as a way to improve their circumstances. For Fatima, it is a way of feeling valued and being seen for something other than her disability; for Asha, regular affairs with political movers and shakers provide her with 'money and power' (p.150), which she values more than the moral standards her family wishes she would abide by.

Dreams

For Karam, hope exists in a carefully nurtured dream of a new home away from the slum. He actively pursues his dream, putting a deposit on the land in Vasai, but he has little capacity to follow through on it; and since his family do not wholeheartedly share this dream, it seems doomed even before Fatima's tragic death takes place.

Suicide

In a confronting representation of individuals' choices in Annawadi, two young adults commit suicide during the narrative, and the reactions indicate that suicide is far from rare in this environment. Both Meena and Sanjay are faced with unbearable futures, and neither have the resources or support to change them. Instead, they choose suicide because from their perspectives it is a valid escape from their painful existence. Boo does not condone these choices, showing them as tragic, and painful for those left behind; however, she presents the events as carefully considered attempts by the characters to take charge of their own destinies.

Even Fatima, although far more impulsive than Meena and Sanjay, is not condemned by Boo for her actions (which lead to her death, although it is not entirely clear whether this was her intention). Rather, the text presents the context within which she made her choice, showing that from some desperate perspectives, death can seem the only hope of escape.

Luck and lack of agency

Key quotes

> 'It seemed … that in Annawadi, fortunes derived not just from what people did, or how well they did it, but from the accidents and catastrophes they dodged.' (p.xx)

While there are numerous instances of characters in Annawadi finding ways to work towards their goals or, at the very least, sustain hope in difficult circumstances, the parallel idea in the text is that most of the characters lack agency over their circumstances and futures. No matter how hard they try, they are still at the mercy of those more powerful, and also of fate. Though many characters strive for improvement, most fail, and many run out of energy. Sunil sums this up in describing how all his efforts have come to nothing, so that he eventually decides to try 'stopping my mind' (p.243) and not even think about self-improvement. Although he idly considers this to be another strategy, since 'maybe then something good could happen' (p.243), there is little evidence of this coming true, and Abdul judges him, revealing his own loss of idealism due to the long-running court cases against his family.

Boo argues that no amount of hard work, religious faith or moral fortitude can insure against the cruelties of fate. This is demonstrated clearly by the way in which the Husains have little control over the outcome of their trial. Though they are not guilty as accused, though they attempt to do the right thing (such as fulfilling Abdul's obligations to check in at Dongri after his release) and though they are a hardworking and relatively honest family, when it comes to their judicial outcomes, Abdul explains, 'the matter was one of many in his life that he considered out of his hands' (p.201).

Another character who illustrates the idea that luck is the dominant factor in individuals' experiences is Asha. The unfairness of Asha's treatment in Chapter 4 by the Corporator – who demands that she gather people at a certain hour, but does not turn up – emphasises the difficulty of life in the slums, even for those such as Asha, who have some power and authority. Yet it also emphasises the role of pure luck, since when she finally speaks to him on the phone in the middle of the night, she receives credit for the noise in the background (the excitement over the eunuch – nothing to do with her) rather than the criticism she had anticipated.

Asha's good fortunes are rarely linked to 'good' behaviour: she manipulates her daughter for her own benefit, cares more about her own wellbeing than any of the slum-dwellers she ostensibly represents, and does not object to the levels of corruption necessary to rise to power. Yet – despite some periods of despair, such as in Chapter 16 – she seems to achieve both power and financial success, insofar as such things are possible in a slum. This complicates the text's view that one's fate is rarely linked to one's actions: while her rewards do not follow positive values or actions, they do frequently follow her own determination and sustained efforts.

Other examples of characters whose fortunes are dictated by luck – either good or bad – in the text include:

- Kalu, who dies despite having recently abandoned stealing and become 'good and improved' (p.164)
- Rahul, who is fortunate enough to secure some hotel work, even though he self-identifies as lazy and fails in his schoolwork.

Alliance

Key quotes

'"It's easy to break a single bamboo stick, but when you bundle the sticks, you can't even bend them," she told her children.' (p.77)

'... powerless individuals blamed other powerless individuals for what they lacked.' (p.237)

The positive relationships in *Behind the Beautiful Forevers* are rarely described as 'friendships'; more often, the relationships in Annawadi are based on mutual benefit and might rather be characterised as alliances. This notion of alliance refers to connections between individuals, such as between Asha and the Corporator, as well as to association within groups, such as those based on common religious faith.

Alliance is a complicated value as presented in this text. Boo shows it to be important, because it is present at all levels – from the lowliest to the politicians – and also because central characters such as Abdul desire it. However, it rarely brings significant benefit to Annawadians and instead is often fraught with challenge. Indeed, the text actually argues that poverty discourages alliance.

Fatima and Zehrunisa

Fatima 'alternately relied on and resented' Zehrunisa (p.72), going crazy after overhearing Zehrunisa criticise her, yet turning to Zehrunisa for support during her fights with her husband (p.77). Similarly, even though Fatima causes the Husains' downfall, Zehrunisa is loyal to her neighbour after her death – largely due to their shared Muslim faith – and not only washes Fatima's corpse but also gives her the Husains' best quilt in which to be buried. This strange camaraderie between two women who seem to despise each other represents a rarity in the slum: the bonds of religious faith are shown to be stronger than those of poverty. (See 'Poverty' for further discussion of this notion.) As Zehrunisa has taught her children, 'despite the petty differences, Muslims have to join up' (p.77), whether in suffering or celebration.

Sunil and other scavengers

Abdul and other scavengers Sonu and Kalu attempt to influence Sunil's habits (tooth-brushing, rising early, giving up smoking; they even tell him which god to favour), but Sunil remains true to himself, though thriving on companionship and comradeship with Abdul and, later, Sonu. Abdul views Sunil with a sceptical fondness, as a 'weird and decent kid' (p.244). The alliances among some of the young scavengers are portrayed as positive but transient.

Lack of alliance among the poor

In Annawadi, poverty is a common enemy, yet the residents of the slums 'rarely got mad *together*' (p.237). Rather, the text demonstrates the conflict that poverty can foster among fellow sufferers. The incident with Fatima and the Husains is a central illustration of this idea that 'poor people didn't unite; they competed ferociously amongst themselves for gains as slender as they were provisional' (p.237). Boo identifies this as a symptom of 'the age of global market capitalism', where individual pain gets in the way of 'common predicament' (p.237).

Manju and Meena

The exception to this notion of unhealthy alliance is the relationship between Manju and Meena. The two girls depend on each other for emotional support, and despite the restrictions on them – Manju's busy schedule and Meena's servitude and lack of freedom – they take time to share their hopes and fears about marriage and a sustainable life. For Meena, sustainability becomes impossible, and Manju mourns her friend, showing a tenderness few other characters exhibit.

Power and corruption

Key quotes

'The Indian criminal justice system was a market like garbage ... Innocence and guilt could be bought and sold like a kilo of polyurethane bags.' (p.107)

'... a doctor entered the room with the results of the forensic investigation. Abdul was seventeen years old if he paid two thousand rupees, and twenty years old if he did not.' (p.129)

'They would go to prison if enough of the supposed witnesses backed Fatima's revised hospital statement to the police about being throttled and beaten.' (p.203)

Corruption is ever-present in both the domestic and the public spheres of Annawadian life, and Boo suggests that this culture of corruption is endemic in the Indian system of power and government. The text illustrates the idea that corruption is a means to power. Corruption is a transactional arrangement where each party needs something from the others, and while those with money are usually in control, they often have needs that can be fulfilled, and leveraged, by the poor.

Evidence of corrupt interactions in the text ranges from the dynamics of relationships to events that affect characters' lives. These include:

- Asha's interactions with the Corporator – she is obliged to support his corrupt political and business dealings in order to maintain her power in the slum
- the Tamil man who runs the game shed and hires out tools to scavengers, obligating their return services
- large-scale governmental dealings that involve 'insider trade' – these include public infrastructure and funding arrangements, international relations and schemes for social support (p.138)
- the underlying corruption and lack of feasibility in the schemes to rehouse slum-dwellers when slums are destroyed
- Sister Paulette and the orphanage, who sell on food that is donated to them for the orphans
- the many extortion attempts Poornima Paikrao makes against the Husains during their case.

Another domain in which corruption is rife is the law enforcement and justice department. The nearby Sahar police station, where much of the Husains' case is handled, is 'not a place where victimhood was redressed and public safety held dear' (p.169). Rather, police are openly discriminatory (both in regards to race and wealth); they solicit and offer bribes to influence their decisions and actions (such as in their arrangement with Kalu in Chapter 10); and they both threaten and enact extreme violence: 'beatings, though outlawed in the human rights code, were practical, as they increased the price the detainees would pay for their release' (p.107). Despite all this, officially 'the Sahar police precinct was among the safest places in Greater Mumbai' (p.168) – largely because of the corruption and distortion in the reporting of crime. In one unusual instance of slight compassion over corruption, however, the officer Thokale seems to feel empathy for the blackmailed Husains and, as Zehrunisa recognises, 'could have taken so much more money than he did' (p.109) in his bribe from them.

The text argues that, in such a flawed national culture of dishonesty, individuals have little alternative but to embrace the corruption, finding ways to turn it to their advantage. Asha is one character who appears to manage this, understanding the economy of bribes and corruption, and engaging with it in order to further her ambitions. She even finds it easy: 'becoming a success in the great, rigged market of the overcity required less effort and intelligence than getting by, day to day, in the slums'; it simply requires luck and an inclination towards the self-delusion that 'what you were doing wasn't all that wrong' and 'you weren't all that likely to get caught' (p.228).

Relative morality

Key quotes

'Though he had obeyed his father all his life, he wasn't about to hit a disabled woman.' (p.94)

'Road boys didn't mind deception; extravagant fabrications passed the time.' (p.163)

'He wanted to be better than what he was made of. In Mumbai's dirty water, he wanted to be ice.' (p.218)

A value in the text closely connected to the theme of power and corruption is that of morality, or what individuals believe to be ethical and good behaviour. A common question in *Behind the Beautiful Forevers* is how far individuals will go to achieve their needs or desires. Often it is the younger characters – still in a position of shaping their futures and personalities – who struggle with this question. A clear illustration of this generational difference in morality is Asha and Manju. Manju dislikes her mother's dishonest dealings, although she is aware that she herself benefits from them: Asha's wheeling and dealing provides the finances to support Manju's education. Manju constantly has to balance her loyalty and obligation to her mother with her own beliefs about what is acceptable. For example, she resents the fact that she will inherit her mother's latest corrupt money-making scheme, yet understands perfectly well it is only through this scheme that Asha is able to afford a computer for her, and this in turn enables her further study (pp.228–9).

Abdul is the other character portrayed as considering moral imperatives. Abdul's decision to become 'better and more honorable' (p.132) at the end of Part Two provides a strong contrast with the practices of corruption that most people in Annawadi and surrounds – even the 'friendly doctor' at Dongri (p.130) – have had to adopt in order to survive. Abdul's moral transformation is one of the key elements of his journey, and again reminds us that poverty is not always a barrier to personal growth.

However, Abdul's transition does not bring the hoped-for rewards, and before long he is demoralised and jaded: he wants to tell The Master that 'he had tried to be honorable in his final years as a boy, but wouldn't be able to sustain it now that he was pretty sure he was a man' (pp.240–1). He feels hopeless, resigning himself to the fact that morality does not provide an escape from poverty. As Sunil once observed about Sonu, he was 'probably the most virtuous boy at Annawadi, but he also had a mother and younger siblings working to supplement the household income' (p.194). The text suggests that morality, while admirable, is a luxury out of reach to those existing within a thoroughly corrupt system – particularly those living in poverty in such a system.

The text also raises the question of *relative* morality: if it is impossible, in the midst of crippling poverty, to aspire to moral behaviour, perhaps it is still worth trying to be comparatively *better*. This is illustrated in Boo's refusal to attribute blame in her descriptions of the incidents surrounding the burning. While Abdul always asserts that he is 'innocent' (p.216), and readers are encouraged to empathise with the Husains in the court case, the family also did verbally abuse Fatima: a fact they never deny. In a country where it is illegal to incite someone to suicide, can they really be considered 'innocent'? And if they are not, does their role in the tragedy justify the treatment they receive? Boo helps us answer these questions by showing that morality is not black and white in an environment such as Annawadi, but rather that it is possible to behave either more or less honourably than others.

DIFFERENT INTERPRETATIONS

Different interpretations arise from different responses to a text. Over time, a text will give rise to a wide range of responses from its readers, who may come from various social or cultural groups and live in very different places and historical periods. Responses by critics and reviewers can be published in newspapers, journals and books, both online and in print. They can also be expressed in discussions among readers in the media, classrooms, book groups and so on.

While there is no single correct reading or interpretation of a text, it is important to understand that an interpretation is more than a personal opinion – it is the justification of a point of view on the text. To present an interpretation of a text based on your point of view, you must use a logical argument and support it with relevant evidence from the text.

The critics' viewpoints

As is the case with many award-winning books, the commercial reviews for *Behind the Beautiful Forevers* have been largely positive, commending Boo's detailed investigations and the literary sensibility with which she conveys the results. Many of the reviews also address similar aspects of the book, in terms of content, construction and style; for example, the impact of poverty, the central event of Fatima's immolation and its aftermath, Boo's research methodology and the novelistic style of the text are frequently discussed in reviews. However, most also feature discussions of specific areas that interest or stand out to the particular reviewer.

Novelist VV Ganeshananthan, in her critique for the *Columbia Journalism Review* (2012), is one of few reviewers not to structure her response to the text by concentrating on Fatima's burning, instead illuminating Boo's interest in the young people of Annawadi. Julian Liam, on the other hand, in his review for the *Los Angeles Review of Books*

(2012), focuses on the context for the book: how Boo became interested in Annawadi and conducted her research, and where the book sits within the genre of creative nonfiction and the existing literature on Indian experiences.

Amit Chaudhuri in *The Guardian* (2012) offers a review from an Indian national's perspective. Chaudhuri, an award-winning Indian writer, was initially cynical about an American journalist's ability to accurately understand and convey such an inherently Indian experience as life in a Mumbai slum. However, his review highlights Boo's research into poverty in her own country, drawing connections between the two subjects and noting that *Behind the Beautiful Forevers* enables readers to see that the issues of poverty are of global relevance and concern, further concluding that Boo's 'novelist's intelligence' manages to override his concerns about her foreigner's perspective. The quality and genre of the writing, for Chaudhuri, are worthy of the sensitive issues Boo has chosen to tackle in her content.

Laila Lalami, a novelist, reviews *Behind the Beautiful Forevers* very positively in independent American journal *The Nation* (2012), and finds it suitable that the text never tries to pose solutions to the systemic problems it identifies: 'it is to [Boo's] credit that she never suggests policies for helping Annawadians out of poverty'. Rather, what Lalami values is the deeply researched exposé on the lived experience of those who are suffering. Like Chaudhuri, she draws links between the Annawadi experience and poverty in other parts of the world, such as America and Morocco. Both these reviewers identify global poverty as a central theme in the book, while commending its local focus on individuals in one small slum.

The New York Times' 'Sunday Book Review' (2012), by Pankaj Mishra, concentrates on the political and social dimensions, also commending Boo's choice to remove her journalistic voice from the narrative perspective, while an article in *One Pakistan* online (2012), which does not identify an author, instead explores some of the Annawadians' responses to the release of the book. The coverage of numerous other publications, such as *The Hindu* online, took the form of an interview with Boo rather than (or in addition to) reviewing the work. This shows the common interest in the research and construction of the text, above and beyond the serious and important subject matter.

Two possible interpretations

The following interpretations demonstrate how even directly contrasting viewpoints about a text can be valid, as long as they are supported with evidence from that text.

Reading 1: *Behind the Beautiful Forevers* shows that life in an Indian slum is unbearable.

Katherine Boo's nonfiction work documents the horrors of slum life in Annawadi, Mumbai, concentrating on the miserable lives of a handful of its residents over a period of several years. Without exception, all of the Annawadian characters struggle to survive, living in extreme poverty in an overcrowded environment where services are limited or non-existent, corruption is rife and competition for basic resources is extreme. Boo's central characters represent a wide range of ages, religious and political associations, castes and family histories, as well as both genders and also hijras or eunuchs (sometimes considered to defy gender definitions). The fact that suffering is a universal experience in the slum, regardless of characters' identities and backgrounds, demonstrates that life in an Indian slum is unbearable.

The forms of suffering experienced in Annawadi are many and varied. The poverty levels mean that access to basic necessities – including clean water, sanitation and shelter – is difficult, and this in turn leads to severe health problems for many residents. Such problems include tuberculosis and heart troubles, and local health services are rife with corruption (Mr Kamble, for example, is expected to pay at least sixty thousand rupees for heart surgery at a public hospital, where such operations are supposed to be provided almost for free). Even when individuals can afford such treatment – as in the case of Fatima or Karam Husain – the hospitals are hopelessly under-resourced, lacking proper doctors, nurses and even medicines.

The struggle to earn any kind of living in an Indian slum is also shown to be horrific: only six of the three thousand slum-dwellers in Annawadi have permanent jobs (p.6), and the rest will do almost anything to earn money. Many labour hard at jobs that are dangerous and unrewarding. Young women are expected to manage housework for large families, often in addition to studying and contributing to the family income. Even the hardworking Abdul Husain, whose family is considered to be wealthy by slum standards, earns a wage that leaves him well below the poverty line. Conflicts such as that between Abdul and his neighbour Fatima – resulting in a drawn-out, unfair legal case – are not uncommon, and support is almost non-existent.

There is almost nothing in the text to show any relief from the pressures of slum life. One small example is the annual festival, Navratri, that Meena and Manju look forward to as a 'flirtfest' (p.180) and an opportunity to dance and party. Yet, tellingly, this sole festive event in the narrative is aborted by the terrible tragedy of Meena's suicide, suggesting that there can be no pleasure for slum-dwellers. Similarly, a small domestic celebration (Asha's birthday) is interrupted by Asha's departure to engage in not only corrupt but also unfaithful activities, leaving her family, especially her daughter Manju, in distress.

Perhaps the strongest argument for the unendurable nature of life in an Indian slum is the suicides that take place in the text: evidence that for many slum-dwellers, life has become literally unbearable. Only two are detailed – those of Sanjay and Meena – but the descriptions of them and reactions to them indicate that this is far from an uncommon response to attempting to survive an Indian slum.

Reading 2: In *Behind the Beautiful Forevers*, Katherine Boo demonstrates that hope and ambition can emerge in even the direst poverty.

While Boo presents a world where life seems unbearable, she populates it with characters who are ambitious, entrepreneurial, resourceful, tenacious and, ultimately, hopeful. Events and characters in her book illustrate how sometimes, far from silencing ambition, difficult circumstances can in fact amplify it.

Annawadian life is full of the daily struggle to survive overcrowding, poverty and, often, conflict or violence. Young men such as Abdul Husain are forced to abandon school in order to support large families when a father is absent or chronically unwell. Young women such as Manju and Meena must obey their parents, sometimes being subjected to abuse as well as unreasonable workloads. Older characters such as Fatima, Mr Kamble and the Husains do not have it any easier. Yet a recurrent theme in the book is the lengths Annawadians will go to in order to improve their lives and their future opportunities.

For example, many of the young people in the slum value their education and attend school diligently or continue their studies even when work commitments keep them away from classes. Manju, for instance, intends to become Annawadi's first female college graduate, and her dedication to her studies – despite her punishing work and domestic schedules – is evidence of the strength of her ambition and the likelihood of her success.

Even the older Annawadians, beyond the age at which they can hope to improve their prospects through education, demonstrate resourcefulness, commitment and determination to achieve goals and ambitions. Examples are Mr Kamble's quest to raise the money for his heart surgery, or Asha's incessant campaign to become slumlord and to make money and gain power in whatever way she can.

In fact, there are several key incidents showing that ambition can arise directly from the tragedies of slum life. These include Abdul's determination to become a more moral person after meeting The Master in the Dongri detention centre, the opportunities for Zehrunisa and Asha when they are forced to take responsibility for their families thanks to ineffectual husbands and the way Mirchi rises to the challenge of supporting his family when Abdul no longer can, after Fatima's death and the resulting accusation. Even Fatima, though it is not admirable behaviour, acts on her ambitions to better herself, seeing in the argument on the maidan an opportunity to improve her prospects.

QUESTIONS & ANSWERS

This section focuses on your analytical writing on the text, and gives you strategies for producing high-quality responses in your coursework and exam essays.

Essay writing – an overview

An essay on a literary work is a formal and serious piece of writing that presents your point of view on the text, usually in response to a given topic. Your 'point of view' in an essay is your interpretation of the meaning of the text's language, structure, characters, situations and events, supported by detailed analysis of textual evidence.

Analyse – don't summarise

In your essays it is important to avoid simply summarising what happens in a text.

- A **summary** is a description or paraphrase (retelling in different words) of the characters and events. For example: 'Macbeth has a horrifying vision of a dagger dripping with blood before he goes to murder King Duncan.'
- An **analysis** is an explanation of the real meaning or significance that lies 'beneath' the text's words (and images, for a film). For example: 'Macbeth's vision of a bloody dagger shows how deeply uneasy he is about the violent act he is contemplating, and conveys his sense that supernatural forces are impelling him to act.'

A limited amount of summary is sometimes necessary to let your reader know which part of the text you wish to discuss. However, always keep this to a minimum and follow it immediately with your analysis of what this part of the text is really telling us.

Plan your essay

Carefully plan your essay so that you have a clear idea of what you are going to say. The plan ensures that your ideas flow logically, that your argument remains consistent and that you stay on the topic. An essay plan should be a list of **brief dot points** – no more than half a page.

Include your central argument or main contention – a concise statement (usually in a single sentence) of your overall response to the topic. See 'Analysing a sample topic' for guidelines on how to formulate a main contention. Write three or four dot points for each paragraph indicating the main idea and evidence/examples from the text. Note that in your essay you will need to *expand* on these points and *analyse* the evidence.

Structure your essay

An essay is a complete, self-contained piece of writing. It has a clear beginning (the introduction), middle (several body paragraphs) and end (the last paragraph or conclusion). It must also have a central argument that runs throughout, linking each paragraph to form a coherent whole. See examples of introductions and conclusions in the 'Analysing a sample topic' and 'Sample answer' sections.

The introduction establishes your overall response to the topic. It includes your main contention and outlines the main evidence you will refer to in the course of the essay. Write your introduction *after* you have done a plan and *before* you write the rest of the essay.

The body paragraphs argue your case – they present evidence from the text and explain how this evidence supports your argument. Each body paragraph needs:

- a strong **topic sentence** (usually the first sentence) that states the main point being made in the paragraph
- **evidence** from the text, including some brief quotations
- **analysis** of the textual evidence, with **explanation** of its significance and how it supports your argument
- **links back to the topic** in one or more statements, usually towards the end of the paragraph.

Connect the body paragraphs so that your discussion flows smoothly. Use some linking words and phrases such as 'similarly' and 'on the other hand', though don't start every paragraph like this. Another strategy is to use a significant word from the last sentence of one paragraph in the first sentence of the next.

Use key terms from the topic – or synonyms for them – throughout, so the relevance of your discussion to the topic is always clear.

The conclusion ties everything together and finishes the essay. It includes strong statements that emphasise your central argument and provide a clear response to the topic.

Avoid simply restating the points made earlier in the essay – this will end on a very flat note and imply that you have run out of ideas and vocabulary. The conclusion should be a logical extension of what you have written, not just a repetition or summary of it. Writing an effective conclusion can be a challenge. Try using these tips:

- Start by linking back to the final sentence of the second-last paragraph – this helps your writing to flow, rather than leaping back to your main contention straight away.
- Use synonyms and expressions with equivalent meanings to vary your vocabulary. This allows you to reinforce your line of argument without being repetitive.
- When planning your essay, think of one or two broad statements or observations about the text's wider meaning. These should be related to the topic and your overall argument. Keep them for the conclusion, since they will give you something 'new' to say but still follow logically from your discussion. The introduction will be focused on the topic, but the conclusion can present a wider view of the text.

Essay topics

1 "In India, a land of few safe assumptions, chronic uncertainty was said to have helped produce a nation of quick-witted, creative problem-solvers." To what extent does *Behind the Beautiful Forevers* support this idea?

2 How does Boo's use of figurative language in *Behind the Beautiful Forevers* develop the theme of hope?

3 'Katherine Boo argues that corruption is an inescapable human behaviour.' Discuss.

4 '*Behind the Beautiful Forevers* presents a world where there is no justice.' Discuss.

5 'Abdul is a victim in the world of Annawadi.' Do you agree?

6 '*Behind the Beautiful Forevers* shows that it is possible to escape one's circumstances.' Discuss.

7 How does Boo use factual evidence to engage the reader?

8 'Alliances are essential to survival in Annawadi.' Discuss.

9 'Asha is a good parent.' Does the text support this assertion?

10 '*Behind the Beautiful Forevers* demonstrates that family and society exert equal pressure on individuals' sense of agency.' Discuss.

Vocabulary for writing on *Behind the Beautiful Forevers*

Creative nonfiction: a genre in which factual events, situations and characters are reported in a literary style.

Maidan: a square or public open space in a community.

Purdah: the social practice in certain Muslim and Hindu societies whereby women are secluded from men.

Self-immolation: a term for setting oneself on fire, which Fatima does.

Slumlord: a landlord or person who owns property in a slum; slumlords typically charge exorbitant rents and provide sub-standard accommodation to their tenants.

Analysing a sample topic

"In India, a land of few safe assumptions, chronic uncertainty was said to have helped produce a nation of quick-witted, creative problem-solvers." To what extent does *Behind the Beautiful Forevers* support this idea?

First, identify the *type* of question: is it asking you to discuss an assertion about the text? Analyse a character? Respond to a possible interpretation of a theme? In this case, you are being asked to discuss how the text illustrates a particular idea: that poverty breeds innovation. The prompt also includes a quotation from the text – make sure you are familiar with its location (p.219) and understand its context, as this will help you address the prompt accurately. Identify key terms in the quotation that will help focus your discussion on appropriate aspects of the text. In this case, key terms might include 'India', 'chronic uncertainty' and 'quick-witted, creative problem-solvers', although you may identify others – key terms can differ for different readers.

The instruction, the second part of the prompt, in this case invites you to make your own decision about how the text reflects the quotation, and allows you to answer in terms of degree: it is not simply an agree/disagree response that is expected (although you may choose to answer with a firm agree/disagree perspective). Again, key terms will help guide you in your understanding of how to approach the topic: here they are 'to what extent', 'support' and, of course, the text title.

Once you understand what the question is asking of you, you will need to form a main contention: the central argument around which your essay will revolve, and in this case an answer to the question posed in the prompt. (Some prompts do not contain direct questions, so you may wish to formulate your contention differently.)

This particular prompt is quite detailed, containing a long quotation about the text and a complex question relating to it. Don't forget that you must address both parts of the topic – your answer to the question must take into account the specific stimulus provided in the quotation, as well as allowing you to explore broader themes and ideas in the text.

In this case, a main contention that affords some nuance is likely to generate a stronger essay. For example, 'Boo's text suggests that the instability of Indian slum life leads individuals to find inventive survival strategies – though these are not always successful', will give you more scope than '*Behind the Beautiful Forevers* does / does not support the idea that necessity is the mother of invention'.

Sample introduction

> Annawadi exemplifies the systemic uncertainties and challenges of life in a country with a fast-growing economy yet high rates of poverty. Boo's nonfiction text *Behind the Beautiful Forevers* explores the lives of a number of slum residents, demonstrating that in such circumstances, those who are capable of creative problem-solving may find opportunities to survive, if not thrive. However, Boo also argues – using factual, detailed examples from Annawadians' lives – that despite the best efforts of individuals to shape their own futures, extreme poverty can thwart even the most energetic, bright and fortunate individuals.

Body paragraph outline

Paragraph 1 – discuss and provide evidence of India as a 'land of few safe assumptions' in the text:

- Annawadi shows how the most underprivileged have no certainty and cannot rely on the democracy or social support of their local or national community.
- Systemic, endemic corruption means Indians – particularly those living in slums – are wisest to assume the most dangerous circumstances (as Abdul argues when he talks about fate, p.xx).
- Include specific examples of the above, such as the unfair treatment the Husains receive in the police department and justice system.

Paragraph 2 – explain what is meant by 'creative problem-solving' in the context of the book:

- Slum-dwellers are faced with a daily struggle to survive (and to resist the temptations of suicide); there are no social supports, so individuals and families must generate their own means of income and sustenance.
- Individuals find ways to work outside, or identify niches in, existing systems and structures.

Paragraphs 3 and 4 – provide examples of both successful and unsuccessful innovations, such as:

- the Tamil game-shed owner devising his own way to capitalise on the scavengers' needs
- Sunil's discovery of the ledge above the river, and his (profitable, as it happens) decision to risk collecting garbage there
- Asha's numerous schemes – some successful and others not – involving political corruption, brokering and loyalties
- Fatima's attempt to blackmail the Husains, which is an example of an individual making the most of a difficult situation in order to profit; unfortunately, her strategy backfires drastically.

Sample conclusion

> In the undercity world of poverty portrayed by Boo, long-term social, political and economic instability has created vastly uneven financial distribution. For those living in the deeply problematic slums of India, often the only way to survive – let alone prosper – is to find or create unconventional means of supporting themselves. However, *Behind the Beautiful Forevers* also demonstrates that there is some mythology to the notion that hardship creates opportunity and innovation. Rather, most Annawadians either fail in such endeavours or conclude that it is pointless to even try, resorting to death rather than attempting to generate solutions.

SAMPLE ANSWER

How does Boo's use of figurative language in *Behind the Beautiful Forevers* develop the theme of hope?

Although it is a nonfiction text, Katherine Boo's *Behind the Beautiful Forevers* harnesses many techniques common to other forms, such as poetry or fiction, enabling her to create not only a factual and concrete portrait of life in a Mumbai slum but also a personal and subjective view of what it is like to live in Annawadi. Although there is much suffering in the slum, there is also much strength and determination. Figurative language helps connect readers emotionally with a text, allowing Boo to engage her readers on a personal as well as an academic level, thus increasing their ability to understand the arguments and points of view she constructs.

Boo's immersive research style and literary journalism come together in the creation of this text. The unusual genre known as creative nonfiction allows her to present the real-world issues with which she is concerned – such as the distribution of wealth and opportunity – with both the accountability of documentary and the subjective, emotive, intimate style of fiction. She constructs characters and situations with rich symbolic and figurative language, including personification, simile and metaphor. For example, 'Annawadians now spoke of better lives casually, as if fortune were a cousin arriving on Sunday', or 'Sunil was a seed of a boy'. These descriptions help readers conceptualise Annawadi as a real place rather than a statistic, and its residents as dynamic, unique individuals.

One of the common traits among many Annawadians is the persistence of hope despite the constant disappointment and destruction that slum life can bring. This is a central theme in Boo's text, and although it is closely linked to the statistical and sociological phenomenon of extreme poverty, it is not a concrete idea that can be addressed or analysed through traditional journalistic writing. Instead, Boo harnesses literary techniques well suited to communicating the abstract and emotional inner lives of characters.

Hope manifests differently in different characters. In Karam, for example, it rests in the dream of a plot of land in Vasai, where his children may be happier, and where a dirt road is 'giddy with chickens' – a figurative rather than a literal description of the landscape. The imagery created is appropriate to Karam's 'dream': evocative and non-literal, like a dream. Conversely, Zehrunisa scorns this dream, and Boo uses figurative language to illustrate this too: Karam's wife demands to know where their children will live in Vasai, in a 'ghost house?' Again, the language choice allows Zehrunisa to clearly articulate how she feels about Karam's dream: it is intangible and unreal.

Sunil, another character who holds hopes of a better future, is often energetically vocal in his assessment of his surroundings. When he sees a map of the world, he is entranced, and 'talked about that map as if it were a gold brick he'd found in the gutter' – for him, the idea of the wider world is a surprising, sparkling, valuable discovery. Later, when he accepts his forced new life of thievery, he at last achieves one of his greatest hopes: 'as a thief, Sunil Sharma had finally started to grow'. Although this description is concrete, referring to his physical size (about which he has been worried since his younger sister outgrew him), it also symbolically indicates his improved financial prospects at this point in the narrative – his growth is not only literal. This use of such layered meaning within language helps to add depth to Sunil's character, in turn developing the related theme of fulfilling ambition.

One of the strongest uses of imagery in the text is Abdul's argument that he wants to become ice in the dirty waters of Mumbai – to become better than what he is made from and what surrounds him. This figurative illustration of his ambitions is a powerful one, and is revisited when his hopes are dashed and his confidence eroded as he continues to await his trial date. He imagines visiting his hero, The Master, and confesses that he is failing to 'keep the ice inside me from melting … I'm just becoming dirty water, like everyone else'. This moment illustrates evocatively the sense of hopelessness Abdul feels, in a much more powerful way than a merely factual description of his mental state would.

Boo's use of rich figurative language throughout *Behind the Beautiful Forevers,* particularly when addressing emotional themes such as the notion of hope under the pressures of poverty, is an example of careful authorial decisions to match form with content. The use of figurative language such as simile and metaphor, commonly associated with the more abstract storytelling of fiction or poetry, encourages readers to engage emotionally with the characters and situations, thus gaining an extra level of understanding of Boo's themes and concerns.

REFERENCES & READING

Text

Boo, K 2012, *Behind the Beautiful Forevers*, Scribe Publications, Melbourne.

Other resources

Reviews

Chaudhuri, A 2012, '*Behind the Beautiful Forevers: Life, Death and Hope in a Mumbai Slum* by Katherine Boo – Review', *The Guardian*, 29 June, https://www.theguardian.com/books/2012/jun/29/behind-beautiful-forevers-katherine-boo-review

Lalami, L 2012, 'In Annawadi: On Katherine Boo', *The Nation*, 7 May, https://www.thenation.com/article/annawadi-katherine-boo/

Mishra, P 2012, 'Fighting for Scraps', *The New York Times*, 9 February, http://www.nytimes.com/2012/02/12/books/review/katherine-boos-behind-the-beautiful-forevers-explores-a-mumbai-slum.html?_r=0

Interviews

'Katherine Boo on Immersion Reporting From a Mumbai Slum' 2013, Radio National, 4 January, http://www.abc.net.au/radionational/programs/mediareport/katherine-boo-on-immersion-reporting-from-a-mumbai-slum/4386476

McGrath, C 2012, 'An Outsider Gives Voice to Slumdogs: Katherine Boo on Her Book *Behind the Beautiful Forevers*', *The New York Times*, 8 February, http://www.nytimes.com/2012/02/09/books/katherine-boo-on-her-book-behind-the-beautiful-forevers.html?_r=0

'Q&A with Katherine' 2012, http://www.behindthebeautifulforevers.com/qa-with-katherine/